BRITN SPEARS

Biography

DEEP IN THE HEART

CONTENTS

CHAPTER 13: I WANT TO BE FREE

CHAPTER 14: PURSUIT OF FREEDOM

CHAPTER 1

CHILDHOODS

I sang my entire childhood. On the drive to dance class, I sang along with the radio. I used to sing when I was depressed. Singing was spiritual to me. I was born and raised in McComb, Mississippi, and now live in Kentwood, Louisiana, about 25 miles away. Hearing our cleaner sing in the laundry room was the first time I was actually moved and felt shivers down my spine. I was always in charge of the family laundry and ironing, but when times were better financially, my mother would hire someone to assist her. The housekeeper sang gospel music, and it was like waking up on another planet. It's something I'll never forget. My desire to sing has gotten stronger since then. Singing is a magical experience. I own who I am when I sing. I can communicate completely. When you sing, you stop saying "Hi, how are you..." You have the ability to say far more significant things. Singing transports me to a mystical realm. My family has a history of tragedy. My middle name is derived from my father's mother, Emma Jean Spears, also known as Jean. I've seen photos of her, and I can see why everyone believed we looked alike. They both have blond hair. The same grin. She appeared to be much younger than she was. My grandfather, June Spears Sr., was abusive to her. Jean had a baby who died when he was only three days old. June committed Jean to Southeast Louisiana Hospital, a dreadful institution near Mandeville, where she was put on lithium. My grandmother Jean shot herself with a shotgun on her infant son's grave in 1966, just over eight years after he died. I can't imagine how sad she must have been. In the South, men like June are described as having "nothing was good enough for him," being "a perfectionist," and being "a very involved father." I'd probably put it even harsher than that. June, a sports fanatic, made my father exercise until he was exhausted. No matter how exhausted or hungry my father was after basketball practice, he still had to shoot a hundred more baskets before he could come inside. June was a Baton Rouge Police Department officer who eventually had ten children with three women. And, as far as I know, no one has a kind word to say about his first fifty years. Even in my family, it was said that the Spears men were bad news, particularly when it came to how they handled women. June didn't confine Jean to a mental institution in Mandeville. He also sent his second wife there. June sexually molested one of my father's half sisters from the age of eleven until she fled away at sixteen, according to one of my father's half sisters.

Jean died on that grave when my father was thirteen. I know that trauma contributed to my father's behaviour with my siblings and me; why nothing was ever good enough for him. My father encouraged my sibling to participate in sports. He drank until he was unable to think. He'd vanish for days at a time. My father was incredibly cruel when he drank. June, on the other hand, softened as he grew older. Instead of the terrible guy who had abused my father and his siblings, I encountered a grandfather who appeared patient and gentle.

My parents married and moved into a tiny house in Kentwood. My mother's relatives no longer supported her, thus my parents were impoverished. My parents were also young—my mother was twenty-one and my father was twenty-three. Bryan, my older brother, was born in 1977. They bought a little three-bedroom ranch house after leaving their previous small place. My mother returned to school to become a teacher when Bryan was born. My father, who worked as a welder at oil refineries—hard jobs that could last a month or three—began to drink heavily, and it was soon taking its toll on the family. According to my mother, a few years after their marriage, my grandfather Barney, my mother's father, died in a vehicle accident, and in the aftermath, my father went on a binge, missing Bryan's first birthday celebration. My father got drunk at a Christmas party when Bryan was a toddler and went missing on Christmas morning. My mother had had enough at that point. She moved in with Lily. She filed for divorce in March of 1980. But June and her new wife asked her to return him, and she did. Everything appeared to be tranquil for a time. My father quit welding and founded a building company. Then, after much effort, he established a gym business as well. When I was four, I was sitting on the couch in our living room with my mom on one side and my friend Cindy on the other. Kentwood was like a soap opera town—there was constant drama. Cindy was telling my mother about the newest scandal as I was listening in and trying to keep up when the door burst open. I could tell something terrible had happened based on the boy's expression. My heart rate slowed.

My mother and I began running. The road had recently been repaved, and I was jogging barefoot on the scorching black tar.

"Ow! Ow! Ow!" With each step, I yelped. When I looked down at my feet, I noticed tar on them.

We eventually got to the field where my brother, Bryan, was playing with his neighbourhood buddies. They were attempting to mow some thick grass with their four-wheelers. Because they were idiots, this sounded like a terrific idea to them. They eventually collided because they couldn't see one other through the dense grass. I must have seen everything, heard Bryan cry in agony and my mother scream in terror, but I have no recollection of any of it. I believe God made me black out so I wouldn't recall the anguish and worry, or the sight of my crushed brother's body. He was transported to the hospital by helicopter. Bryan was in a full body cast when I went to see him a few days later. He'd shattered practically every bone in his body, from what I could see. As a kid, the fact that he had to pee through a hole in the cast sealed the deal for me. Another thing I couldn't help but notice was that the entire room was crammed with toys. My parents were so thankful he'd lived and so sorry for him that every day of his recovery felt like Christmas. My mother catered to my brother out of guilt. Even today, she defers to him. It's amazing how one short second can forever alter the dynamics of a family. My brother and I grew closer as a result of the accident. Our friendship was developed as a result of my real recognition of his anguish. When my father began regular drinking, his enterprises began to disintegrate. My father's frequent mood swings added to the weight of not having money. I was especially nervous about being in the car with my father because he would talk to himself while driving. I couldn't understand what he was saying. He seemed to be lost in his own world. Even back then, I could see why my father wanted to drown himself in drink. Work was causing him anxiety. June, I can see how he was self-medicating after years of trauma at the hands of his father. But I couldn't figure out why dad was so hard on us at the time, why nothing we did seemed to be enough for him. The most heartbreaking thing was that all I ever desired was a parent who would embrace me for who I was—someone who would say, "I just love you." Right now, you have the ability to do anything. I'd still adore you no matter what.``

My father was reckless, cold, and cruel to me, but he was even worse to Bryan. He was ruthless in pushing him to succeed in athletics. Bryan's life was far more difficult than mine during those years since our father subjected him to the same strict schedule that June had imposed on him. Despite his physical restrictions, Bryan felt impelled to play basketball and football. My father, who was more of a drinker who would vanish for days at a time, could also be abusive to my mother. To be honest, his leaving benefited us. I liked it when he was not present. My mother would argue with him all night, making his time at home even more terrible. He couldn't speak since he was so drunk. I doubt he could even hear her. But we might be able to pull it off. Bryan and I were forced to face the consequences of her rage, including the inability to sleep through the night. Her screams rang out throughout the house.

"Just feed him and go put him to bed!" In my nightgown, I'd stomp out into the living room. He's sick!"

She was fighting someone who was completely unaware. But she would not listen. I'd go back to bed, scowling at the ceiling and cursing her in my heart as I listened to her yell. Isn't it awful? He was the one who was drunk. He was the one whose alcoholism had contributed to our poverty. He was the one who had collapsed in his chair. But it was she who bothered me the most, because he was quiet during such times. I needed to sleep badly, but she wouldn't stop chatting. Regardless of the nightly turmoil, my mother made our house a place where my friends wanted to hang out—at least when my father respected us enough to drink elsewhere. Everyone in the neighbourhood showed up. Our house was the cool house, for lack of a better phrase. We set up a tall bar with twelve chairs surrounding it. My mother was a typical young Southern mother, frequently chattering and smoking cigarettes with her friends at the bar (she smoked Virginia Slims, the same cigarettes I now smoke) or on the phone with them. All of them thought I was dead. The older kids sat in the bar stools in front of the television, playing video games. I was the youngest, and I didn't know how to play video games, so I had to compete for the older kids' attention. Our house looked like a zoo. When Bryan was little, my mother would run after him, hopping over sofas to get him so she could swat him when he back-talked her. I was always ecstatic, trying to divert the focus of the older kids away from the TV in the living room or the grownups away from each other in the kitchen.

"Britney, stop!" my mother would yell. "We have visitors!" Just be respectful. Maintain your finest demeanour."

But I prefer to disregard her. And I could always keep everyone's attention.

CHAPTER 2

COMPETITIONS

I was little and quiet, but when I sang, I came alive, and I had enough gymnastics training to move effectively. I entered a local dance competition when I was five years old. My skill was a dance routine performed while wearing a top hat and twirling a cane. I won. My mother then began taking me to contests all around the region. I'm sporting the most outrageous outfits in previous photos and videos. I dressed like a Christmas present in my third-grade musical, wearing a loose purple T-shirt with a giant purple bow on top of my head. It was truly dreadful. I worked my way up the talent circuit, eventually winning a regional competition in Baton Rouge. Before long, my parents had their sights set on bigger chances than what we might achieve by collecting prizes in school gymnasiums. They suggested we go when they read an announcement in the papers for an open call for The All New Mickey Mouse Club. We drove to Atlanta for eight hours. There were over 2,000 children present. I had to stand out, especially since we later discovered that they were only seeking for children above the age of ten. When the casting director, Matt Casella, asked my age, I opened my lips to respond "Eight," then remembered the age-ten threshold and said, "Nine!" He gave me a suspicious glance.

I auditioned by singing "Sweet Georgia Brown" while performing a dance routine that included gymnastics flips. They whittled down a group of thousands of youngsters from across the country to a handful of kids, including Keri Russell, a gorgeous girl from California a few years older than myself. Christina Aguilera, a girl from Pennsylvania, and I were told we didn't make the cut but that we were talented. Matt stated we'd be able to get on the show if we were older and more experienced. He suggested to my mother that we travel to New York City for work. He suggested we find an agent he respected who helped young actors get started in the theatre.

We did not leave right away. Instead, I stayed in Louisiana for approximately six months and started to work, serving tables at Lexie's seafood restaurant, Granny's Seafood and Deli, to help out.

The eatery had a foul, fishy odour. Nonetheless, the cuisine was incredible—indescribably excellent. And it quickly became the new hotspot for all the kids. In high school, my brother and his pals would get drunk in the deli's back room. Meanwhile, I was washing shellfish and serving plates of food on the floor at the age of nine, while performing my prissy dancing in my lovely little clothes. My mother sent a video of me to Nancy Carson, the agent Matt had recommended. In the video, I sang "Shine On, Harvest Moon." It worked: she invited us to meet with her in New York. We got back on the Amtrak and proceeded home after I sang for Nancy in her workplace twenty stories up in a building in Midtown Manhattan. A talent agency had officially signed me.

Jamie Lynn, my younger sister, was born not long after we returned to Louisiana. Laura Lynne and I spent hours in the playhouse pretending she was one of our dolls. I was getting ready for a dance competition a few days after my mother returned home with the baby when she began acting strangely. She was hand-sewing a rip in my outfit, but she got up and threw it away while she was manipulating the needle and thread. She didn't appear to understand what she was doing. To be honest, the costume was a shambles, but I needed it to compete.

"Mama! "Why did you throw away my costume?" I inquired.

Then there was blood all of a sudden. There was blood everywhere.

Something had not been correctly sewed up after she gave delivery. She was dripping with blood. I cried out for my father. "What's wrong with her?" I exclaimed. "What's wrong with her?"

Daddy arrived and drove her to the hospital. "Something cannot be wrong with my mom!" I yelled the entire journey. I was nine years old. A river of blood gushing out of your mother would be upsetting for anyone, but it was horrific for a youngster that age. I'd never seen so much blood in my life. When we arrived at the doctor's office, they had her mended in what seemed like two seconds. Nobody appeared really bothered. Postpartum haemorrhage appears to be rather common. But it stayed with me. I'd constantly look to see if my mom was on the other side of the window, waiting for me to finish gymnastics class. It was a reflex that I had to perform in order to feel protected. But one day, when I went out the window to check in, she wasn't there. I became terrified. She'd gone. She has vanished! Perhaps indefinitely! I burst into tears. I knelt on my knees. You'd think someone had died if you saw me.

My teacher came running over to console me. "Honey, she's going to come back!" she exclaimed. "It's all right! She most likely went to Walmart!"

My mother had, in fact, done just that: she had gone to Walmart. But it was not acceptable. I couldn't bear the thought of her going. She never left that window during class again after seeing how unhappy I was when she returned. And she never left my side for the following few years. I was a young girl with huge ambitions. I want to be a celebrity such as Madonna, Dolly Parton, or Whitney Houston. I had simpler ambitions as well, dreams that appeared even more difficult to fulfil and felt too ambitious to express aloud: I want my father to stop drinking. I'd like my mother to stop yelling. I want everything to be well. With my family, anything might happen at any time. I had no authority there. Only while I was performing did I feel completely invincible. At least one thing was fully within my control as I stood in a Manhattan conference room in front of a woman who could make my fantasies come true.

I was invited to be a participant on Star Search when I was ten years old.

At the first event, I sang a spirited rendition of a Judy Garland song called "I Don't Care." I received 3.75 stars. My opponent, an opera singer, received a 3.5. I moved on to the next round. The second show was taped later that day, and I was up against Marty Thomas, a twelve-year-old bolo-tie-wearing boy with a lot of hair spray in his hair. We were amicable, and we even played basketball before the show. I sang the Judds' "Love Can Build a Bridge," which I'd performed at my aunt's wedding the year before.

Marty and I were interviewed onstage by the host, Ed McMahon, while we waited for our scores.

"I noticed last week, you have the most adorable, pretty eyes," that's what he said to me. "Do you have a boyfriend?"

"No, sir," I replied.

"Why not?"

"They're mean."

"Boyfriends?" Ed stated. "Do you mean that all boys are mean?" I'm not a jerk! "What about me?"

"Well, it depends," I responded.

"I get that a lot," Ed admitted.

I received 3.75 once again. Marty received a perfect score of 4. Ed wished me well as I walked away after I smiled and hugged him gently. I kept it together until I got backstage, at which point I fell into tears. My mother then got me a hot fudge sundae.

My mother and I continued to fly back and forth to New York. As a young girl, the intensity of working in the city was both fascinating and scary. I was offered a role as an understudy in Ruthless!, an off-Broadway musical inspired by The Bad Seed, All About Eve, Mame, and Gypsy. Tina Denmark, a psychotic child star, was the character I played. Tina's first hit was "Born to Entertain." It was really close to home. Natalie Portman, a promising young actress, was the other understudy.

While I was performing in the play, we rented a small apartment near my public school, the Professional Performing Arts School, for my mother, Jamie Lynn, and myself, and I took courses nearby at Broadway Dance Center. But I usually spent my time at the downtown Players Theatre. In some ways, the experience was a confirmation, proof that I had the talent to make it in the theatrical world. However, it was a demanding schedule. I didn't have time to be a normal youngster or develop friends because I had to work virtually every day. There were two shows on Saturdays. I also disliked being an understudy. Every night, I had to be at the theatre until as late as midnight in case I had to fill in for the main Tina,

Laura Bell Bundy. She left after a few months, and I took over as leader, but I was exhausted. By the time Christmas rolled around, I was desperate to get home—until I discovered I was slated to perform on Christmas Day. "Am I really going to do this for Christmas?" I questioned my mother, in tears. I glanced at our tiny apartment tree, picturing the robust evergreen we'd have in our living room in Kentwood.

In my little-girl thinking, I couldn't fathom why I'd want to do that—perform during the holidays. As a result, I left the show and went home. The New York City theatre schedule was simply too demanding for me at the time. But one good thing came out of it: I learnt how to sing in a venue with poor acoustics. The audience is right alongside you—there are just 200 individuals in the room. To be honest, it's funny, but singing feels more electrifying in that atmosphere. The intimacy you feel with the members in the audience is unique. Their excitement energised me. With that experience under my belt, I tried out for the Mickey Mouse Club again. While waiting to hear about the Mickey Mouse Club in Kentwood, I became a basketball point guard at Parklane Academy. I was small for an eleven-year-old, but I could run the plays. People think I was a cheerleader, but I was never one. I dabbled in dancing on the side, but in school, I wanted to play ball, so I did despite my height. I wore a gigantic number 25 jersey that was far too big for me. I was a tiny mouse zipping around outside. For a while, I had a crush on a fifteen or sixteen-year-old basketball player. He hit every three-point attempt and made it seem effortless. People would travel long distances to see him play, just as they had to see my father. He was good—not as brilliant as my father had been, but nonetheless a ball genius. I was awestruck by him and my friends who were taller than me. My move was to grab the ball from an opponent player in mid-dribble, race down the court, and make a layup. I like the rush of quickly weaving around the opposing team. The adrenaline of not having a script and the play being spontaneous and utterly unknown made me feel so alive. No one noticed me coming because I was so small and charming. It wasn't the same as being onstage in New York City, but it seemed like the next best thing under the bright lights of the court, waiting for the sound of applause.

My second audition for the Mickey Mouse Club resulted in a booking. Matt, the pleasant casting director who had suggested my mother to our agency, Nancy, thought I was ready.

Being in the program was like boot camp for the entertainment industry: there were long dance rehearsals, singing lessons, acting workshops, recording studio time, and school in between. The Mouseketeers rapidly splintered into cliques, separated by the dressing rooms we shared: Christina Aguilera and I were the younger kids, sharing a dressing room with another girl, Nikki DeLoach. We looked up to the older kids, like Keri Russell, Ryan Gosling, and Tony Lucca, who I thought was quite attractive. And I rapidly became acquainted with a young man named Justin Timberlake.

We were shooting at Disney World in Orlando, and my mother and Jamie Lynn, who was two at the time, had joined me. During the day, the cast would go on rides and have a good time. It was truly a child's dream—incredibly entertaining, especially for a kid like myself. But it was also extremely difficult work: we would run choreography thirty times a day, attempting to master every move.

The only downer was learning that my grandmother Lily had died not long into filming. She perished in the pool while swimming, maybe as a result of a heart attack or stroke. We couldn't afford to go home for Justin's funeral, but Lynn Harless, Justin's generous mother, agreed to lend us the plane ticket. It was something that a family would do, and the children and adults on that show were like family.

Tony walked into our changing room one day while seeking a hat that a wardrobe guy had left in the girls' room. When he walked in, my heart dropped out of my chest. He was my romantic interest. I couldn't believe he'd just entered my dressing room! My small heart dropped to the ground.

At another sleepover, we played Truth or Dare, and someone challenged Justin to kiss me. As he leaned in and kissed me, a Janet Jackson song was playing in the background. It transported me back to third grade, when I was holding a guy's hand for the first time in the library. It was the most important thing to me because it was so genuine and powerful. That was the first time someone had shown me any romantic interest, and it felt like a fantastic rebellion. We'd been watching a movie and had hidden our hands beneath the desk so the teachers couldn't see.

The Mickey Mouse Club was a fantastic experience that got my feet wet in the world of television. Performing on that show sparked my interest. I knew then that I wanted to do what I did there—sing and dance. When the show finished a year and a half later, many of my castmates moved to New York or Los Angeles to pursue their goals. But I chose to return to Kentwood. There was already a push-pull within me: half of me wanted to keep working toward the dream, while the other part wanted to live a normal life in Louisiana. I had to let normalcy reign for a moment. Back at home, I returned to Parklane, settling into typical adolescent life—or the closest thing to "normal" that my family allowed. Starting in eighth school, my mother and I would take the two-hour journey from Kentwood to Biloxi, Mississippi, just for fun, and drink daiquiris. Our beverages were dubbed "toddies." I liked being able to drink with my mother on occasion. We didn't drink in the same way my father did. He became more depressed and shut off when he drank. We became happier, more alive, and more daring. Trips to the beach with my sister were some of my favourite times with my parents. I'd sip a little teeny White Russian while we drove. The drink tasted like ice cream to me. That was my slice of heaven when it had just the right amount of shaved ice, cream, and sugar, but not too much alcohol. My sister and I both had matching bathing suits and perms. Giving a young child a perm is now practically prohibited, but it was adorable back in the 1990s. Jamie Lynn was a living doll at three, the craziest, most adorable child ever. So that was our focus. We'd go to Biloxi, drink, relax on the beach, and return delighted. And we had a good time. We had a great time. Even in the midst of all the sadness, there was a lot of joy in my childhood.

I began drinking with my mother and smoking with my pals by the age of thirteen. I smoked my first cigarette at the home of one of my "bad" friends. All of my other pals were nerds, but this one was popular: her sister was a senior, she always wore the nicest makeup, and guys flocked to her. She led me to a barn and gave me my first cigarette. Despite the fact that it was only tobacco, I felt high. I recall wondering to myself, "Am I going to die?" Is this sensation going away? When will this sensation vanish? I want another cigarette as soon as I finish my first. I did a decent job of concealing my habit from my mother, but one day she had me drive us home from the store along the long road that led to our house—I started driving at thirteen, too—when she suddenly began sniffing the air.

"I smell smoke!" exclaimed her. "Have you been smoking?"

She quickly snatched one of my hands off the steering wheel and drew it to her to smell. I lost control of the steering wheel as she did this, and the car spun off the road. Everything seemed to be happening in slow motion. When I turned around, I noticed Jamie Lynn pressed backward into the seat: she was wearing a seat belt but wasn't in a car seat. I kept thinking, We're going to die, as we spun what felt like extremely slowly. We're going to die. We're going to die. Then, bang! The car's buttocks collided with a telephone pole. It was a miracle that we hit so hard. We would have gone through the windshield if we had hit the pole while moving ahead. My mother stepped out of the car and began yelling—at me for crashing, at cars passing by for assistance, and at the universe for allowing this to happen. Fortunately, no one was injured. We all got up and walked away. Even better, my mother had forgotten about how she had caught me smoking. Is smoking in my adolescence a crime? Whatever. We were on the verge of death! She never mentioned it again after that. Some sixth-grade boys at school asked me to go smoke a cigarette in their locker room during break. They only ever asked one girl to join them, and I was the only one who said yes. I've never felt more relaxed. The boys' locker room, thankfully, had two doors, one of which led outside. I recall us jamming the door open so the smoke could escape and we wouldn't be discovered. It became a habit. But it didn't last long. After a while, I decided to give it a shot without the boys. My best friend and I went to smoke in the girls' locker room this time, but there was only one door. We were discovered red-handed and taken to the principal's office.

"Were you smoking?" inquired the principal.

"No!" I exclaimed. My best friend covertly reached down and pinched my hand so hard. The principle clearly didn't trust me, but guess what? We got away with just a warning. "I swear to God, Britney, you're the worst liar I've ever seen in my life," my pal later stated. Please let me do the talking next time."

By that age, I wasn't simply drinking and smoking; I was also precocious when it came to boys. I had a huge crush on one of the guys who was often hanging out at the house of my "bad" friend. He was about eighteen or nineteen years old, and he had a tomboy girlfriend at the time. They were definitely the "it" pair at our school. I wished he'd glance at me, but I didn't hold out much hope given that I was five years his junior. I was sleeping over at my "bad" friend's house one night. The guy I had a crush on snuck into the house in the middle of the night—it had to be three a.m.—with no notice. I was asleep on the couch when I awoke to see him sitting next to me. He began kissing me, and soon we were making out on the couch. What is going on? I pondered. It was like a séance—as if I'd summoned him! I couldn't believe it when my crush appeared out of nowhere and began making out with me. And it was delicious. All he did was kiss me. He made no other attempts. I liked a lot of the males in my brother's group that year. Bryan was a funny kid—weird in the greatest way. But as a senior, he rose to become the school's monarch, a total badass. During his senior year, I began dating his closest buddy and lost my virginity to him. I was in ninth school, and the guy was seventeen. My involvement with him took up a lot of my time. I would arrive at school at seven a.m. as usual, then leave at lunchtime, around one p.m., to spend the afternoon with him. Then he'd drive me back just as school was ending. I'd just hop on the bus and go home as if nothing had occurred. My mother eventually received a call from the school office; I'd missed seventeen days and would have to make them up.

"How did you do it?" my mother said. "How did you leave?"

"Oh, I forged your signature," that's what I said.

The age difference between me and that person was plainly enormous—now it seems outrageous—and my protective older brother began to despise him. Bryan spotted me sneaking out to visit his friend and informed our parents. As punishment, I had to wander around the neighbourhood with a bucket all day, cleaning up garbage like a highway prisoner. Bryan followed me about, snapping pictures of me picking up trash as I was crying. Aside from those instances, there was something so sweetly typical about that time in my life: going to homecoming and prom, driving around our small town, and going to the movies. But, in reality, I missed performing. My mother had contacted a lawyer she'd met on my audition circuit, Larry Rudolph, whom she would occasionally call for business assistance. He suggested I make a demo after she emailed him footage of me singing. He had a song called "Today" that Toni Braxton had recorded for her second album but had left on the editing room floor. He sent me the song, which I learnt before recording it in a studio an hour and a half away in New Orleans. This would be the demo I'd use to get my foot in the door at record labels. At the same time, Justin and another Mouseketeer, JC Chasez, were members of the newly formed boy band NSYNC. Another castmate, Nikki, with whom I'd shared that dressing room, was planning to join a girl group, but after consulting with my mother, we opted to go solo instead. Larry played the demo for some executives in New York who expressed interest in seeing what I could do. So I put on my tiny heels and pretty little outfit and went back to New York. I had attempted to return to being a normal adolescent, but it had failed. I was still looking for something more.

CHAPTER 3

THE BEGINNING OF SUCCESS

Who exactly is this man? I thought about it. I'm not sure, but I appreciate his place of work and his dog. He was just a little old man, but he was full of vitality. I estimated his age to be approximately 65 (he was in his fifties). Larry had told me the man's name was Clive Calder, and he was an important contact. I had no idea what he was up to. I would have been more terrified if I had realised he was a record executive who founded Jive Records. Instead, I was simply fascinated. And I fell in love with him the instant I met him. He worked in a scary three-story building. And there was a teacup terrier in the office—a species of dog I had no idea existed—who was the smallest, cutest thing I'd ever seen. I felt like I was in another world when I walked in and saw that office and that dog. Everything shifted into another dimension. I walked into a fantastic dream.

"Hi, Britney!" he shouted, almost quivering with joy. "How are ya?"

He pretended to be a powerful secret club member. He spoke with a South African accent, making him sound like a character from an old movie. I'd never heard somebody speak like that in real life.

He allowed me to pick up his dog. As I cradled the tiny animal in my arms and looked over the vast office, I couldn't stop smiling. My dreams took off from there. I hadn't recorded anything other than the demo. I was just going to see the people Larry had recommended I see. I was aware that I was due to perform a song for record industry officials. And I knew I wanted to be around that guy more, and that the way he was influenced how I wanted to be. I'm not surprised if he was my uncle in another life. I was constantly drawn to him. It was his grin. Wise, astute, and astute. He had a strange smile on his face. It's something I'll never forget. I had so much fun with him that I thought the trip to New York was more than worthwhile, even if all it gave me was the opportunity to meet someone like that, someone who believed in me. But my day wasn't done yet. Larry drove me across town, and I sang Whitney Houston's "I Have Nothing" in front of an audience of executives. As I glanced out at rooms full of men in suits staring at me in my short dress and high heels, I sang loudly. Clive quickly signed me. So, at fifteen years old, I signed a recording contract with Jive Records.

The label needed me in the studio as soon as possible. They set Fe and me up in a New York apartment. Every day, we'd travel to New Jersey, where I'd sing in a booth for producer and songwriter Eric Foster White, who'd previously worked with Whitney Houston. To be honest, I had no idea. I had no idea what was going on. I just knew I loved to sing and dance, and whatever gods could come down and organise it for me, I'd be there. If someone could put something together for me that presented me in a way that others could relate to, I was ready. I'm not sure what happened, but God worked his magic, and there I was, recording in New Jersey.

The booth where I sang was underneath. When you're inside, all you can hear is yourself singing. That was something I did for months. I didn't leave the booth. I went to a cookout at someone's place after working hard. At the time, I was really girly, constantly wearing a dress and shoes. I was there talking with folks and trying to make a good impression when I hurried to grab Felicia and bring her out on the balcony. I had no idea there was a screen door there. I rushed right into it, slammed it with my nose, and stumbled backwards. Everyone looked up when they noticed me on the floor, holding my nose.

I swear to God, when I say I was humiliated...

When I stood up, someone said to me, "You know there's a screen there."

"Yeah, thanks," I responded.

Everyone, of course, just laughed their little fannies off.

I felt really humiliated. Isn't it strange that out of all that happened to me throughout that first year of recording, that was one of my most distinct memories? That was more than 25 years ago! I was heartbroken! But, to be honest, I was more surprised because I had no idea that the screen was there. It made me think I'd been recording in the booth for far too long. Things were coming together for my debut record about a year into my tenure in New Jersey. Then one of the execs said to me, "You need to meet this Swedish producer." He's fantastic. He composes catchy music."

"All right," I replied. "Who has he worked with?"

I'm not sure how I knew to ask that question, given my inexperience, but I'd begun to have distinct notions about how I wanted to sound. I also conducted some research and discovered that at the time, he'd written songs for the Backstreet Boys, Robyn, and Bryan Adams.

"Yes," I said. "Let's do it."

Max Martin went to New York for a dinner meeting with only me and him, no aides or label officials present. Despite the fact that I was typically accompanied by handlers due to my age, they wanted me to meet him alone in this situation. As we sat, a waiter approached and asked, "How may I assist you?"

A candle accidentally flipped over, igniting the entire table. We were in one of New York City's most expensive restaurants, and our table had suddenly turned into a wall of fire—from "How may I assist you?" to a flame wall in less than a second.

Max and I exchanged horrified looks. "Should we leave now?" he asked.

He was a wizard. And we began to collaborate.

I flew to Sweden to record songs, but the difference between there and New Jersey was barely discernible: I was just in another booth.

"Do you want some coffee?" Felicia would ask. Let's go get some fresh air!"

I'd shake her off. I laboured for hours on end. My work ethic was excellent. I'd never come out. You wouldn't hear from me for days if you knew who I was back then. I would spend as much time as I could in the studio. If someone wanted to leave, I'd tell them, "I wasn't perfect."

I was listening to Soft Cell's "Tainted Love" the night before we recorded "... Baby One More Time" and fell in love with that sound. I stayed up late to arrive at the studio weary and with my voice fried. It was successful. When I sang, it came out gravelly, sounding more mature and sexier. I became obsessed with the recording once I realised what was going on. And Max was attentive. He understood what I meant when I stated I wanted more R&B in my voice and less plain pop, and he made it happen. When all of the songs were finished, someone said, "What else can you do?" "Do you want to dance right now?"

"Do I want to dance?" I asked. I certainly do!"

The label approached me with an idea for a video for "... Baby One More Time" in which I would portray a futuristic astronaut. The mock-up I saw depicted me as a Power Ranger. That image didn't resonate with me, and I suspected my audience wouldn't either. I told the label executives that I felt people would want to witness my friends and me sitting in school, bored, and then starting dancing as soon as the bell rang.

The choreographer had us moving so smoothly. The fact that the majority of the dancers were from New York City helped. There are two camps in the realm of pop dance. Most individuals believe that LA dancers are superior. No offence, but my spirit has always preferred New York dancers because they have more heart. We practised at Broadway Dance Center, where I had taken classes as a child, so I was familiar with the facility. I turned it on for Jive Records executive Barry Weiss when he arrived at the studio. I demonstrated my abilities to him at that time.

Nigel Dick, the video's director, was open to my suggestions. In addition to the school bell signalling the start of the dancing, I stressed the importance of there being cute boys. When we started dancing outside in our normal clothing, I felt we should wear school uniforms to make it appear more thrilling. Miss Fe was even cast as my teacher. I thought it was hilarious to see her in geeky glasses and drab teaching garb.

Making that video was the most enjoyable aspect of making that first record. That was perhaps the point in my life when I was most passionate about music. I was unknown, and if I messed up, I had nothing to lose. Being anonymous provides a great deal of flexibility. I could gaze out at an audience that hadn't seen me before and thought to myself, "You don't know who I am yet." It felt liberated to know that I didn't have to worry about making mistakes. It wasn't about posing and smiling for me when I was performing. I felt like a basketball player driving down the court onstage. I had street awareness as well as ball sense. I had no dread. I knew just when to take my shots.

Beginning in the summer, Jive sent me on a mall tour—to around twenty-six malls! That type of promotion is not enjoyable. Nobody knew who I was at the time. I had to try to sell myself to people who were uninterested in me. My demeanour was genuine—it wasn't an act. I had no idea what I was doing. I'd just say, "Hey, hello!" My music is fantastic! You have to look into it!"

Before the video, not many people knew what I looked like. However, by the end of September, the song was being played on the radio. On October 23, 1998, I was sixteen years old when the single "... Baby One More Time" was released. The video was released the next month, and I was suddenly known everywhere I went. The album was released on January 12, 1999, and it soon sold over ten million copies. In the United States, I debuted at number one on the Billboard 200 list. I was the first woman to have a number one single and album launch at the same time. I was overjoyed. And I could feel my life opening up. I no longer had to perform at shopping malls.

Things were moving quickly. I toured aboard tour buses with NSYNC, including my old Mickey Mouse Club pal Justin Timberlake. My dancers, Felicia, or one of my two managers, Larry Rudolph and Johnny Wright, were constantly with me. Big Rob, a security guard I hired, was incredibly nice to me. On MTV's Total Request Live, I became a regular. Rolling Stone brought David LaChapelle to Louisiana to photograph me for the April cover story, "Inside the Heart, Mind, & Bedroom of a Teen Dream." The images were contentious when they were published since the cover shot of me in my underwear holding a Teletubby highlighted how young I was. My mother was apprehensive, but I was determined to work with David LaChapelle again. Every day was different. I was meeting a lot of interesting folks! I met singer-songwriter Paula Cole at a New York party shortly after "Baby" was released. She was roughly fourteen years my senior. Oh my God, I admired her so much—at first, just because of her appearance. She was the tiniest thing, with the most curly brown hair cascading down her back. I had no notion who she was, only that she was stunning, with an extraordinary look and energy. Years later, I discovered she was also the vocalist of songs I adored. When I initially heard her voice, I assumed she didn't look anything like she did. When she put her angelic face to her super-dirty words on "Feelin' Love," and her petite body with the strength of her voice on "I Don't Want to Wait," I learned how powerful it can be when women defy expectations.

After the Mickey Mouse Club, Justin Timberlake and I stayed in touch and spent time together on the NSYNC tour. We had a shorthand since we had shared that experience at such an early age. We have a lot in common. We met while I was on tour and began hanging out during the day before and after gigs. I quickly recognized that I was absolutely over heels in love with him—so much so that I was pathetically in love with him. When he and I were in the same room, we were like magnets, according to his mother. We'd just run into each other and stick together. You couldn't describe how we were together. To be honest, it was strange how in love we were. Back then, his band, NSYNC, was dubbed "so pimp." They were white boys who liked hip-hop. That's what set them apart from the Backstreet Boys, who seemed to deliberately portray themselves as a white group. NSYNC socialised with Black artists. I thought they tried too hard to blend in at times. J and I were in New York one day, exploring sections of town I'd never seen before. A man with a large, blinged-out medallion was walking our way. He was surrounded by two massive security guards.

J became ecstatic and exclaimed, "Oh yeah, fo shiz, fo shiz! Ginuwine!" "How are you, homie?"

Felicia did a J impersonation after Ginuwine left, saying, "Oh yeah, fo shiz, fo shiz! Ginuwine!"

J wasn't even ashamed. He simply accepted it and stared at her as if to say, "Fuck you, Fe."

That's when he got his first necklace, a large T for Timberlake. I couldn't seem to be as carefree as he did. I couldn't help but observe that the questions he was asked by talk show presenters were not the same as the ones I was asked. Everyone started making bizarre comments about my breasts, wondering if I'd undergone plastic surgery. Press may be awkward, but at award events, I felt pure joy. The child in me got a kick out of watching Aerosmith's Steven Tyler for the first time at the MTV Video Music Awards. I noticed him arriving late, dressed in what appeared to be a wizard's cape. I exclaimed. Seeing him in person felt weird. Lenny Kravitz arrived late as well. And once more, I thought, Legends! Legends are everywhere! I began to run into Madonna all over the world. I'd perform in Germany and Italy, and we'd end up at the same European awards events. We'd greet each other as if we were old friends. I knocked on Mariah Carey's dressing room door at an awards show. When she opened it, the most amazing, ethereal light gushed forth. You know how we all have ring lights these days? Well, more than twenty years ago, only Mariah Carey knew about ring lights. And no, I can't say only her first name. To me she is always going to be Mariah Carey.

I asked if we could take a photo together and tried to take one where we were standing, and she answered, "No! Come stand here, sweetie. This is my brightness. This is my side. I want you to stand here so I can get my nice side, girl." She kept saying that in her deep, gorgeous voice: "My good side, girl. My good side, girl."

I did everything Mariah Carey ordered me to do and we took the photo. Of course she was exactly right about everything—the shot looked amazing. I know I received an award that night, but I couldn't even tell you what it was. The true reward was a beautiful portrait with Mariah Carey.

In the meantime, I was setting records and became one of the best-selling female artists of all time. People started referring to me as the "Princess of Pop."

I sang the Rolling Stones' "(I Can't Get No) Satisfaction" and then "Oops!... I Did It Again" at the 2000 VMAs while changing from a suit and hat to a sparkly bikini top and tight jeans, my long hair down. Wade Robson choreographed it; he always understood how to make me look both strong and feminine. During the cage dance breaks, I struck stances that made me appear dainty in the midst of an intense performance.

Later, MTV put me in front of a monitor and forced me to watch strangers in Times Square rate my performance. Some of them stated I did a fantastic job, but a lot of them seemed to be focused on the fact that I was wearing skimpy clothing. They claimed that I was dressing "too sexy," setting a negative example for children. The cameras were trained on me to watch how I would react to this criticism, whether I would take it well or cry. Did I make a mistake? I was perplexed. I'd just finished dancing my heart out on the awards show. I never claimed to be a role model. I only wanted to sing and dance. The MTV show host persisted. What did I think of the people who said I was corrupting America's youth?

"Some of them were very sweet," I finally said. But I'm not the children's mother or father. I just have to be myself. I know there will be individuals who dislike me—I know not everyone will."

It jolted me. And it was my first true taste of a long-lasting backlash. Every time I turned on an entertainment show, it seemed like someone was criticising me and saying I wasn't "authentic." I was never quite clear what all these critics expected me to do—a Bob Dylan impression? I was a teen from the Deep South. I added a heart to my signature. I enjoyed appearing cute. Why did everyone treat me as if I were dangerous, even when I was a teenager?

Meanwhile, I began to see an increasing number of older males in the crowd, and it freaked me out to see them leering at me as if I were some kind of Lolita fantasy for them, especially since no one seemed to think of me as both sexy and capable, or talented and hot

They appeared to believe I was stupid if I was sexy. I couldn't possibly be talented if I was hot.

I wish I'd known Dolly Parton's joke at the time: "I'm not offended by all the dumb blonde jokes because I know I'm not dumb." I'm also aware that I'm not blonde." My natural hair colour is dark brown.

To guard my heart from criticism and keep my concentration on what was important, I began reading religious works such as Neale Donald Walsch's Conversations with God series. I also began taking Prozac.

When Oops!... I Did It Again was out, I was a household star and in complete control of my career. Around the time of my first world tour with Oops!, I was able to build a house for my mother and pay off my father's debts. I wanted to start over for them.

There was little time to practise. I just had a week to prepare. I was on stage with Aerosmith, Mary J. Blige, Nelly, and NSYNC at the 2001 Super Bowl halftime concert. Justin and the rest of his band wore special gloves that sprayed sparks! I sang "Walk This Way" while dressed in sexy football gear, complete with shining silver slacks, a crop top, and an athletic sock on one of my arms. I was taken to Steven Tyler's trailer immediately before the event to meet him, and his energy was incredible: he was such an idol to me. When we were done, the stadium was lit up with pyrotechnics.

The halftime spectacle was simply one of many pleasant surprises in my life. I was named the "most powerful woman" on Forbes' list of the most powerful celebrities; the following year, I was ranked first overall. I discovered that tabloids were making so much money off my images that I was nearly single-handedly keeping some magazines afloat. And I began to receive incredible offers.

The intention was for me to perform "I'm a Slave 4 U" at the 2001 MTV Video Music Awards in September, with a snake as a prop. It's become an iconic moment in the history of the VMAs, but it was far scarier than it appeared.

I first saw the snake when it was delivered to a small back chamber of the Metropolitan Opera House in Manhattan, where we would be performing the play. The girl who gave it over was even smaller than me—she appeared to be extremely young and had blond hair. I couldn't believe they didn't have a large guy in charge—"You're letting us two little munchkins handle this huge snake?" I thought.

But there we were, and there was no turning back: she hoisted the snake and wrapped it over my head and shoulders. To be honest, I was terrified—that snake was large, yellow and white, crinkly, and disgusting. It was fine because the girl who handed it to me, as well as a snake handler and a slew of other people, were present.

But everything changed when I had to perform the song onstage with the snake. Onstage, I'm in performance mode: I'm dressed up and there's no one else except me. When the little munchkin came to me again and brought me the gigantic snake, all I knew was to look down because I was afraid if I looked up and caught its eye, it would kill me.

In my brain, I was telling myself, "Just perform, just use your legs, just perform." Nobody knows, however, that as I was singing, the snake brought its head right up to my face and began hissing at me. You didn't see that shot on TV, but did you see it in real life? I was thinking to myself, "Are you serious right now?" The tongue of the fucking goddamn snake is flicking out at me. Right. Now. Thank God, I finally got to the part when I handed it back.

The next night, just days before September 11, I performed a duet of "The Way You Make Me Feel" with Michael Jackson to commemorate his solo career's 30th anniversary at Madison Square Garden in New York City. I prowled around the stage in my heels. The audience erupted. At one point, it seemed like the entire crowd of 20,000 was singing along with us.

Pepsi commissioned me to create advertisements for them. In "The Joy of Pepsi," I began as a delivery driver and ended up in a big dance routine. In "Now and Then," I got to dress up in gorgeous costumes from different eras. For the 1980s portion, I dressed up like Robert Palmer and sang "Simply Irresistible." I was in hair and makeup for four hours, and they still couldn't make me look like a man. In the fifties, however, I enjoyed dancing at the drive-in. My hair was like Betty Boop's. Working in all of those diverse genres, I was astounded by how well-thought-out those commercials were.

Crossroads, written by Shonda Rhimes and directed by Tamra Davis, was my debut film. We shot it in March 2001, around the time I was finishing up my album Britney. I played Lucy Wagner, a "good girl" in the film. It wasn't an easy process for me. My issue was not with any of the people engaged in the production, but with what acting did to my head. I believe I began Method acting, but I didn't know how to break out of my persona. I truly transformed into this other person. Some people practise Method acting, but they are usually conscious that they are doing it. But there was no divide between us.

It's awful to admit, but it's as if a cloud or something came over me and I just became Lucy. When the camera turned on, I became her, and I couldn't tell when the camera was on and when it wasn't. That may appear ridiculous, yet that is the truth. That's how serious I took it. I took it seriously enough that Justin asked, "Why are you walking like that? "What is your name?"

All I can say is that Lucy was a sweet child who wrote poems about how she was "not a girl, not yet a woman," and not a serial killer.

I ended up walking differently, carrying myself differently, and speaking differently as a result. For months, I pretended to be someone else while filming Crossroads. I'm sure the females I shot that movie with still think she's a touch... weird. They were correct in their assessment.

Like the character, I was a baby. I should've acted like myself on video. But I was so eager to do a good job that I kept attempting to delve into this character's backstory. I'd been myself my entire life and wanted to try something new! I should have realised it was a teen road movie. It isn't that deep. To be honest, just have fun.

After the film was completed, one of my girlfriends from a bar in Los Angeles came to see me. We went shopping at CVS. I swear to God, I stepped into the store, and as I talked to her while we shopped, I finally realised who I was. When I went outdoors again, the movie's magic had been broken. It was bizarre. My small spirit reappeared in my body. That trip to the makeup store with a buddy seemed like waving a magic wand. Then I became enraged.

Oh my God, what have I been doing for the past few months? What exactly was I?

That was basically the start and conclusion of my acting career, and I was relieved. The Notebook casting came down to me and Rachel McAdams, and while reconnecting with Ryan Gosling after our time on the Mickey Mouse Club would have been wonderful, I'm glad I didn't do it. If I had, instead of working on my record In the Zone, I would have spent my days and nights dressing up as a 1940s heiress. I'm sure a big part of the problem was that it was my first time acting. I'm sure there are folks in the acting industry who have struggled to separate themselves from a character. However, I believe they maintain perspective. I hope I never have to deal with that occupational hazard again. Being half yourself and half a fictional character is a bad way to live. After a while, you're not sure what's real.

When I reflect on that time, I realise I was genuinely living the dream, my dream. My excursions brought me around the globe. One of my favourite tour memories was performing at the Rock in Rio 3 music festival in January 2001. In Brazil, I felt unfettered, almost like a child—a woman and a child rolled into one. At that point, I was fearless, filled with a high and a desire.

My dancers—eight of them, two girls and the rest guys—and I went skinny-dipping in the ocean at night, singing, dancing, and joking with each other. We talked for hours in the moonlight. It was breathtaking. We were exhausted, so we went into the steam rooms and talked some more. I could be a little sinful back then—skinny-dipping, staying up all night talking—nothing too extreme. It tasted like revolt and freedom, but I was just having fun and acting like a nineteen-year-old. My fourth and favourite tour was the Dream Within a Dream Tour, which took place shortly after the release of my album Britney in the fall of 2001. Every night onstage, I had to combat a mirror version of myself, which felt like a metaphor for something. However, such a mirror act was only for one song. There was even some flying! And there's an Egyptian barge! And there's a jungle! Snow! Lasers! Wade Robson directed and choreographed it, and I applaud everyone who worked on it. It was well thought out, in my opinion. Wade saw the play as representing a new, more mature stage in my life. The set and costumes were outstanding. I was always grateful when someone knew exactly how to style me. They were astute in their presentation of me as a celebrity, and I know I owe them. They admired me as an artist because of how they captured me. That tour's creators were outstanding. It was by far my favourite tour. It was just what we had all hoped for. I had worked so hard to get there. I'd done small tours before Baby was published, but the Baby tour was the first time I got to see a large crowd. I recall thinking, "Wow, I'm somebody now." Then Oops! grew in size, and by the time I completed the Dream Within a Dream Tour, everything was magical.

By the spring of 2002, I'd hosted SNL twice, first as a butter churn girl at a colonial reenactment museum alongside Jimmy Fallon and Rachel Dratch, and then as Barbie's younger sister, Skipper, alongside Amy Poehler as Barbie. In the same broadcast, I was the youngest person to host and perform as a musical guest. I was asked if I wanted to be in a movie musical around that time. I wasn't sure if I wanted to act again after Crossroads, but this one persuaded me. It was the city of Chicago. Executives from the production approached me at a performance location and asked if I wanted to do it. I'd turned down three or four films because I was so focused on the stage show. I didn't want to be taken away from the music. I was content with what I was doing. But now that I think about it, I should have done it in Chicago. I had power back then, and I wish I'd utilised it more wisely and rebelliously. It would have been fun to visit Chicago. It's all dance pieces, which are my favourite type: prissy, girlie follies, Pussycat Doll-style, serve-off-your-corset routines. I wish I had accepted the offer. I would have gotten to portray a villain who murders a man while singing and dancing. I could have probably discovered ways, or acquired training, to avoid becoming a Chicago character like Lucy in Crossroads. I wish I'd tried something new. If only I'd been bold enough to step outside of my comfort zone and try more things that weren't only within my knowledge. But I was determined not to disturb anyone and to remain silent even when something irritated me.

In my personal life, I was overjoyed. Justin and I shared an apartment in Orlando. We shared a lovely, light-filled two-story home with a tile roof and a pool in the backyard. Even though we were both working a lot, we tried to spend as much time as we could at home together. I always returned every couple months so Justin and I could spend two weeks, sometimes even two months, together. That was our starting point. My relatives flew down to see us when Jamie Lynn was tiny. We went to FAO Schwarz in Pointe Orlando with a group. They shut down the entire store for us. My sister received a small convertible automobile with working doors. It was something between an automobile and a go-kart. We managed to get it back to Kentwood, where she drove it around the neighbourhood until she outgrew it. This cute little girl, driving around in a small red Mercedes, was unlike anything else. It was the most adorable thing you'd ever seen in your life. The vision was incredible, I swear to God. We were all like that with Jamie Lynn: you see it, you like it, you want it, and you get it. Her world, as best as I could tell, was the Ariana Grande song "7 Rings" come to life. (We didn't have much money when I was growing up. My Madame Alexander dolls were among my most valued belongings. There were dozens of options. Their eyelids moved up and down, and they were all named. Some were fictional or historical personalities, such as Scarlett O'Hara or Queen Elizabeth. I had the Little Women girls. You'd think I'd won the jackpot when I acquired my sixteenth doll!)

That was a happy period in my life. I was head over heels in love with Justin. I'm not sure if love is different when you're younger, but what Justin and I shared was extraordinary. He wouldn't even have to say or do anything for me to be attracted to him. Moms in the South love to gather their children and announce, "Listen, we're going to church today, and we're all going to colour-coordinate." That's what I did when Justin and I went to the American Music Awards, which I co hosted with LL Cool J in 2001. I can't believe Justin was going to wear denim and I suggested, "We should match!" Let's wear denim top denim!"

To be honest, I thought it was a joke at first. I didn't believe my stylist would do it, and I certainly didn't think Justin would do it with me. They both, however, went all in.

Justin's all-denim costume, complete with a denim hat to match his denim jacket and denim leggings, was delivered by the stylist. I was surprised when he put it on. So, we're actually doing this!

Justin and I were constantly attending events together. We had a lot of fun at the Teen Choice Awards, and we frequently colour-coordinated our clothes. But we blew it up with the matching denim. That night, my corset had me squeezed in so tightly beneath my denim gown that I was on the verge of collapsing. I get that it was tacky, but it was also fairly wonderful in its own right, and I love seeing it parodied as a Halloween costume. I've heard Justin get chastised for his appearance. On a podcast, he joked, "You do a lot of things when you're young and in love." That is completely correct. We were ecstatic, and our clothing reflected that. I knew Justin had cheated on me a handful of times during our relationship. I let it go because I was so captivated and in love, even though the tabloids seemed determined to rub it in my face. When NSYNC visited London in 2000, photographers caught him in a car with one of the All Saints females. But I didn't say anything. We'd just been together for a year at the time. Another time, we were in Vegas, and one of my dancers who had been hanging out with him informed me that he'd made a gesture toward a girl and said, "Yeah, man, I hit that last night." I won't disclose who he was referring to because she's actually rather well-known and married with children. I don't want her to be upset.

My friend was taken aback and assumed Justin was merely bragging because he was high. There were reports about his having relationships with several dancers and groupies. I let it all go, although he'd plainly slept around. It was one of those situations where you knew but didn't say anything. I did the same. Not much— just once, with Wade Robson. We went to a Spanish pub one night when we were out. We danced and danced and danced. That night, I had sex with him. For years, I had only had eyes for Justin, with one exception, which I disclosed to him. That night was written off as something that happens when you're as young as we were, and Justin and I moved on and remained together. I assumed we'd be together for the rest of our lives. I was hoping we would be. I became pregnant with Justin's baby when we were dating. It was unexpected, but it was hardly a tragedy in my opinion. Justin was my absolute favourite. I always imagined us having a family one day. This would just be far sooner than I had anticipated. After all, what was done was done.But Justin was displeased with the pregnancy. He stated we weren't ready for a baby and that we were far too young. I could see what you were saying. I mean, I kind of got it. I didn't think I had much of a choice if he didn't want to be a father. I wouldn't want to force him to do something he didn't want to do. Our friendship was far too crucial to me. So, even though I'm sure people will detest me for it, I agreed not to have the baby. Abortion was not something I would have chosen for myself, but given the circumstances, it is what we did. I'm not sure if that was the best decision. I would never have done it if it had been up to me alone. Despite this, Justin was adamant that he did not want to be a father. We also agreed on something that, in retrospect, was, in my opinion, incorrect: I should not go to a doctor or a hospital to have the abortion. It was critical that no one knew about the pregnancy or the abortion, so everything had to be done at home.We even didn't notify my family. Apart from Justin and me, the only other person who knew was Felicia, who was always willing to assist me. Someone said to me, "It might hurt a little bit, but you'll be fine."

I took the pills on the specified day, with only Felicia and Justin there. I soon began to have terrible cramping. I ran into the bathroom and stayed there for hours, sobbing and screaming on the floor. They should have numbed me with something, I reasoned. I desired some form of anaesthetic. I needed to see a doctor. I was terrified. I laid there wondering if I would die. I can't even begin to convey how awful it was. The agony was unbearable. I crouched down on my knees, gripping the toilet. I couldn't move for a long time. It's still one of the most agonising things I've ever gone through in my life. Nonetheless, they did not transport me to the hospital. Justin entered the bathroom and joined me on the floor. He felt music could help at some time, so he got his guitar and lay down with me, strumming it. I sobbed and cried till it was all over. It took hours, and I don't recall how it finished, but I remember the pain and anxiety twenty years later. I was messed up for a while after that, especially because I still loved Justin so much. It was absurd how much I liked him, and it was unfortunate for me. I should have predicted the breakup, but I didn't.

When Justin began working on his debut solo album, Justified, he became increasingly distant from me. I believe it was because he'd decided to use me as fodder for his record, and it was hard for him to be around me staring at him with all that affection and dedication. He eventually ended our relationship via text message when I was on the set of Darkchild's "Overprotected" remix video. I had to go back out and dance after seeing the message while sitting in my trailer between takes. As much as Justin damaged me, there was a strong foundation of love between us, and when he left, I was crushed. When I say I was distraught, I mean I couldn't speak for months. Every time someone asked me about him, all I could do was cry. I'm not sure if I was clinically in shock, but it felt like it.

Everyone who knew me felt there was something seriously wrong with me. When I returned to Kentwood, I was unable to communicate with my family or friends. I had only just left the house. That was my fault. I sat in my bed, staring at the ceiling. Justin travelled to Louisiana to see me. He brought me a framed letter he'd written. It's still under my bed. And at the end, it uttered something that made me want to cry: "I can't breathe without you." Those are the final words. Damn, I thought as I read that. He's an excellent writer. Because that is just how I felt. After everything that had transpired, I almost felt like I was suffocating, like I couldn't breathe. The issue is, even after I saw him and read the message, I couldn't shake the trance. He did everything, he came to see me, and I still couldn't talk to him or anybody else.

CHAPTER 4

HEAL WOUNDS

Even though I didn't want to play, I had tour dates left in my contract, so I went back out to finish them. I just wanted to get off the road: To have the entire day and night to myself. To stroll out onto the Santa Monica Pier, breathe in the salt air, listen to the roller coaster rattle, and gaze out at the sea. Instead, every day was a struggle. Fill up. Load up. Check the volume. Photographic session. "What town are we even in?" he wonders. I used to enjoy the Dream Within a Dream Tour, but it had turned into a chore. I was exhausted both mentally and physically. I wanted to turn everything off. I'd started thinking about owning a small shop on Venice Beach with Felicia and retiring from show business entirely. With the benefit of hindsight, I can see that I didn't give myself enough time to recover from Justin's split.

We headed south in late July 2002, near the end of the trip, to perform in Mexico City. But getting there was nearly impossible. We were riding in vans, and after crossing the border, we came to a halt. We'd been stopped by a group of men with the largest firearms I'd ever seen. I was afraid, like if we were being ambushed. It didn't make sense to me, but all I knew was that we were surrounded by these enraged men. Everyone in my van was tense; I had security, but who knew what would happen? After what seemed like an eternity, there appeared to be some kind of peace discussions taking place, as if in a movie. It's still a mystery to me what transpired, but we were eventually allowed to continue, and we got to play in front of 50,000 people (albeit the second gig, the next day, had to be cancelled halfway through due to a major thunderstorm). That storm-cancelled event was the final date of the Dream Within a Dream Tour, but when I told people after the tour that I needed to recuperate, they were all anxious. When you're successful at something, there's a lot of pressure to continue doing it even if you're no longer enjoying it. And, as I quickly discovered, you can't go home again.

Back in Louisiana, I did an interview with People magazine for reasons that seemed absurd to me: I wasn't marketing anything, but my team thought I should show that I was doing well and "just taking a little break." The photographer photographed me both outside and inside, with the dogs and my mother on the couch. They made me empty my purse to prove I wasn't carrying narcotics or cigarettes: all they discovered were Juicy Fruit gum, vanilla perfume, mints, and a small vial of St. John's wort. "My daughter is doing beautifully," my mother assured the reporter. "She's never, ever been close to a breakdown." Part of what made that time so tough was that Justin's family was the only genuine, loving family I had. I would only spend holidays with his family. I knew his grandmother and grandfather, and I adored them. They reminded me of home. My mother would come out and visit us every now and again, but she was never the person I went home to.

My mother was attempting to heal from her divorce from my father, which she had finally completed; distraught and self-medicating, she could hardly get off the sofa. My father was not to be found. And when I say my little sister was a real b*tch, I'm not kidding. I was always the worker bee. I hadn't been paying attention to what was going on in Kentwood while I was doing my thing on the road with Felicia. But when I returned home, I noticed how things had changed. My mother would bring Jamie Lynn small chocolate milkshakes as she watched TV. The girl clearly dominated the roost. Meanwhile, I felt like a ghost child. I recall stepping into the room and feeling as if no one had noticed me. Jamie Lynn only saw the television. My mother, who had formerly been the person I felt the most connected to in the world, was now on another planet. And the way adolescent Jamie Lynn spoke to my mother made my mouth drop open. "Are you going to let this little witch talk to you like that?" I'd ask my mother as I listened to her spew these terrible comments. I mean, she was terrible. Jamie Lynn's transformation made me feel deceived. I had purchased a home for Jamie Lynn to grow up in. She wasn't exactly overjoyed. "Why'd she get us a house?" she'd later ask, as if it were an inconvenience. But that house was a gift. I'd purchased it because our family needed a new home and I wanted her to have a better life than I had.

Life in Louisiana had slipped away from me. I didn't know who to talk to. Going through that breakup, returning home, and realising how much I didn't fit in anywhere anymore, I understood I was technically maturing, becoming a woman. And yet, in my imagination, it was almost as if I went backwards and became younger at the same time. Have you ever watched the film The

Curious Case of Benjamin Button? That's exactly how I felt. That year, as I became more vulnerable, I began to feel like a child again.

In order to regain my confidence, I travelled to Milan in September 2002 to see Donatella Versace. That journey re-energized me, reminding me that there was still fun to be had in the world. We drank fantastic wine and ate fantastic food. Donatella was an engaging host. I was hopeful that things would start to improve from there. She had asked me to one of her runway presentations in Italy. Donatella clothed me in a stunning dazzling rainbow gown. I was meant to sing, but I didn't feel like it, so after some posing, Donatella said we could take it easy. She played my rendition of Joan Jett's "I Love Rock 'n' Roll," I introduced myself to the models, and we were done. Then it was time to celebrate. Donatella is notorious for throwing extravagant parties, and this was no exception. I remember seeing Lenny Kravitz and other amazing individuals there. That party was truly the first time I put myself out there following Justin's breakup—on my own, naïve. During the party, I observed a guy and thought he was really cute. He appeared to be Brazilian: black hair, beautiful, smoking a blunt—your standard bad boy. He wasn't like the LA actor types I'd met before; he was more like a real man, the kind of man you'd have a one-night stand with. He was only for sex. He was talking to these two girls when I first noticed him, but I could tell he wanted to talk to me. We eventually started communicating, and I planned to meet him for drinks at my hotel. We drove to my car, but he did something that completely turned me off—I honestly can't remember what it was. But there was one small detail that irked me, so I urged the driver to pull over and, without saying anything, I kicked the person out on the side of the road and left him there. Now that I'm a mother, I'd never do something like that—I'd say, "I'll drop you off at this location at this time..." But it was instinct at the time, when I was twenty years old. I'd made a mistake by letting this man into my automobile, so I threw him out.

Justin was set to release his solo album Justified shortly after my return. On 20/20, he sang an unpublished song called "Don't Go (Horrible Woman)" for Barbara Walters, which seemed to be about me: "I thought our love was so powerful. I guess I was completely mistaken. But, on the bright side, at least you provided me with a song about another Horrible Woman."

Less than a month later, he released the video for his song "Cry Me a River," in which a woman who resembles me cheats on him and he wanders around in the rain, depressed. I was portrayed in the media as a harlot who had broken the heart of America's golden boy. The truth was that I was unconscious in Louisiana, while he was gleefully running around Hollywood. May I just add that amid all the hype around his dynamite record, Justin failed to mention the multiple times he'd cheated on me? Men have traditionally had greater leeway in Hollywood than women. And I watch how guys are encouraged to slander women in order to get fame and power. But I was broken. The prospect of betraying him added agony to the record and gave it a purpose: shit-talking an unfaithful lady. A plot with the theme "Fuck you, bitch!" was popular in hip-hop culture at the time. Taking revenge on women for perceived mistreatment was popular at the time. The deadly revenge song "Kim" by Eminem was a tremendous hit. The only difficulty with the story was that it wasn't true in our circumstance. "Cry Me a River" performed admirably. Everyone felt terrible for him. And it embarrassed me.

I thought there was no way to tell my side of the story at the time. I couldn't explain because I knew no one would side with me once Justin had persuaded the world of his story. Justin didn't comprehend how powerful he was in shaming me. I don't think he understands it even now. After "Cry Me a River" came out, I was booed everywhere I went. When I went to clubs, I would hear boos. I once went to a Lakers game with my little sister and one of my brother's pals, and the entire stadium booed me.

Justin told everyone that he and I had a sexual relationship, which some have said painted me as not only a cheating slut but also a liar and hypocrite. Because I had so many adolescent followers, my management and publicity agents had long sought to depict me as an everlasting virgin—despite the fact that Justin and I had been living together and having sex since I was fourteen. Was I upset because he "outed" me as sexually active? No. To be honest, I liked how Justin said that. Why did my management strive so hard to portray me as a young-girl virgin far into my twenties? Who cared whether I'd had sex or not?

I'd enjoyed it when Oprah said on her show that my sexuality was none of their concern, and that when it came to virginity, "you don't need a world announcement if you change your mind."Yes, I contributed to that portrayal as a teenager because everyone was making such a huge deal about it. But, when you think about it, it was very dumb of people to describe my physique in that way, to point to me and say, "Look! A virgin!" It's none of your business. And it pulled the spotlight away from me as a musician and performer. I worked extremely hard on my music and performance acts. But the only questions some reporters had for me were whether or not my breasts were real (they were) and whether or not my hymen was intact. Justin's admission to everyone that we'd had a sexual relationship broke the ice and ensured that I never had to come out as a non-virgin. His mentioning our sex never upset me, and I've defended him to some who have attacked him for doing so. "That's so rude!" people have commented regarding his sexual comments about me. But I enjoyed it. When he stated that, I heard him say, "She's a woman." She is not a virgin. "Be quiet."

I'd always had a guilty conscience, a lot of shame, and a sense that my family felt I was just plain awful as a kid. The despair and loneliness that would strike me felt somehow my fault, as if I deserved misfortune and poor luck. I knew the truth about our relationship wasn't what was being depicted, but I still assumed that if I was suffering, it was because I deserved it. I'd undoubtedly done horrible things along the way. Because I believe in karma, I imagine that when awful things happen, it's just the law of karma catching up with me. I've always been quite sensitive. Even though I'm thousands of miles away, I can sense what folks in Nebraska are feeling. Women's cycles sometimes coincide; I feel like my emotions are always in sync with those around me. I'm not sure what hippie term to use—cosmic consciousness, intuition, psychic connection. All I know is that I can completely sense other people's energy. I can't help but notice it. You could be thinking to yourself at this time, "Oh my God, is she really going to talk about this New Age stuff?"

Just one more minute. Because the point is, I was sensitive, young, and still reeling from the abortion and breakup; I didn't handle things well. Justin framed our time together with me as the bad person, and I bought into it, so I've felt cursed ever since. And yet, if it were true, if I had so much negative karma, it might be up to me—as an adult, as a woman—to reverse my luck, to bring myself good fortune. I couldn't take it any longer and fled to Arizona with a partner. That girlfriend was dating Justin's best buddy, and we'd all split up around the same time, so we decided to take a road trip to get away from it all. We found each other and decided to leave everything behind. My buddy was heartbroken, too, given what she'd gone through, so we chatted a lot, beside ourselves with loss and loneliness, and I was grateful for her friendship.

The sky above us was full of stars as we sped through the desert in a convertible with the top down and the wind in our hair—no music playing, just the sound of the night blasting past us. An unsettling feeling fell over me as we peered out at the road in front of us. I'd been going so quickly for so long that I couldn't catch my breath. Something flooded me just now: a tremendous beauty, otherworldly and humbling. I looked across to my companion, unsure whether I should say anything. But what could I possibly say? "Do you believe in aliens?" So I kept quiet and sat with the feeling for a long time. Then I heard her voice above the din of the wind.

"Do you feel that?" she inquired. She gave me a look. "What is that?"

Whatever it was, she sensed it as well.

I took her hand in mine and squeezed it tightly. Rumi, the poet, says that the wound is where the light enters you. That is something I have always believed. We felt what we felt that night in Arizona because we needed it at the time. We were both spiritually open and spiritually raw. It demonstrated that there was more to life than what we could see—call it God, a higher power, or a paranormal experience. Whatever it was, it was genuine enough for us to share the experience. I didn't want to bring it up with my pal at first since I felt embarrassed. I was afraid she'd think I'd gone insane. I've been frightened to speak up so many times because I was terrified someone would think I was insane. But I had to learn that lesson the hard way. Even if it worries you, you must express what you are experiencing. You must convey your story. You must raise your voice.

That night, when I was lost and felt God in the wilderness, I still had a lot to learn. But I knew I wasn't going to let the darkness engulf me. Even in the darkest night, there is plenty of light.

According to what I heard, Justin slept with six or seven different girls in the weeks following our official breakup. He was Justin Timberlake, after all. This was his first solo trip. He was every girl's fantasy. I was madly in love with him. I could see why people were so taken with him. I decided that if Justin was going to date, I should try to do the same. I hadn't dated in a long time, having been devastated and on tour. That winter, I saw a handsome guy, and a club promoter buddy told me I had good taste.

"That guy is so cool!" exclaimed my companion. "His name is Colin Farrell, and he's shooting a movie right now."

So, speaking of balls, I hopped in my car and drove up to the set of his action film, S.W.A.T. What was I thinking?

There was no security, so I went directly to the soundstage, where they were filming a house set piece. "Come sit in my chair!" urged the director when he spotted me.

"Okay," I replied. So I sat in the chair and waited for them to start shooting. "Do you have any pointers for what I should do here?" Colin said. He was asking me to steer him.

We ended up fighting for two weeks. We were all over each other, battling so furiously that it felt like we were in a street battle. During our enjoyable time together, he took me to the premiere of The Recruit, a spy thriller starring Al Pacino. I was overjoyed when he asked me to accompany him. I was dressed in a PJ top. I believed it was a real shirt because it had little studs on it, but after seeing the images, I realised: Yeah, I certainly wore a full-fledged pyjama top to Colin Farrell's premiere. I was overjoyed to be there for the premiere. Colin's entire family was present, and they were all really kind. I tried to convince myself, like I had before when I was too attached to a man, that it wasn't a huge problem, that we were just having fun, that in this case I was vulnerable because I wasn't over Justin yet. But for a tiny minute, I thought there could be something there. My romantic disappointments were only one factor in how alienated I grew. I was constantly self-conscious.

I tried to be social. Natalie Portman, whom I'd known since we were tiny children on the New York theatre circuit, and I even had a New Year's Eve party. But it took a tremendous lot of effort. On most days, I couldn't even bring myself to call a buddy. I was terrified of going out and being brave onstage or in clubs, or even at gatherings or meals. Joy was uncommon in large groups of individuals. I suffered from severe social anxiety the majority of the time. What appears to most people to be a perfectly regular conversation becomes mortifying to you as a result of social anxiety. Being among people at all, especially at a party or other event where there is an expectation of presenting well, creates surges of humiliation for no apparent reason. I was terrified of being judged or saying something foolish. When that feeling comes over me, I want to be alone. When I'm afraid, all I want to do is excuse myself to the bathroom and then sneak out.

Madonna was one of my few guests during that bizarre, surreal time. She walked into the room and, of course, she immediately owned it. I recall thinking, "This is Madonna's room now." She was stunningly attractive and emanated strength and confidence. She stepped straight to the window and said, "Nice view."

"Yeah, it's a nice view, I guess," he replied.

Madonna's unwavering confidence let me see my position with new eyes. I believe she had an innate grasp of what I was going through. I needed some direction at the moment. I was perplexed about my life. She attempted to coach me. She performed a red-string ceremony with me at one time to introduce me into Kabbalah, and she gave me a trunk full of Zohar volumes to pray with. I tattooed a Hebrew term that means one of God's seventy-two names at the base of my neck. Some Kabbalists see it as healing, which is what I was still attempting to achieve. Madonna had a positive influence on me in many ways. She advised me to make time for my soul, and I attempted to do so. She exemplified the kind of strength I needed to witness. There were so many various ways to be a woman in the industry: you could be a diva, a professional, or just "nice." I had always worked so hard to please—my parents, the audience, everyone. My mother must have instilled in me a sense of powerlessness. I witnessed how my sister and father handled her and how she just accepted it. I adopted that model early in my career and became passive. I wish I'd had a badass bitch mentor back then so I could've learnt how to do that sooner. If I could go back in time, I would attempt to be my own parent, partner, and advocate, much like Madonna. She had faced sexism and bullying from the public and the industry, as well as being embarrassed for her sexuality on numerous occasions, but she had always triumphed. When Madonna won her Billboard Woman of the Year award a few years ago, she stated that she had experienced "blatant misogyny, sexism, incessant bullying, and persistent harassment... You have to play the game if you're a girl. What exactly is that game? You have the right to be beautiful, cute, and sexy. But don't overdo it. "I have no opinion."

She is correct that the music industry—indeed, the entire world—is geared for guys. You can be absolutely ruined, especially if you're "nice," like me. I'd gotten almost too friendly by that time. Felicia would write thank-you letters to the chef, the bartender, and the secretary wherever I went. As a Southern girl, I still believe in a handwritten thank-you note. Madonna noticed how much I wanted to please and how much I wanted to do what others did rather than shutting something down and saying, "OK, everyone! Take note! This is what will happen."

We decided to perform at the VMAs together. We did an air kiss every time we practised. I was sitting on the side of the stage about two minutes before the performance, thinking about my biggest performance yet at the VMAs, when I'd pulled off a suit to unveil a sparkly outfit. I said to myself, "I want another moment like that this year." Should I just go for it with the kiss? That kiss drew a lot of attention. Madonna was asked about it by Oprah. The kiss was seen as a great cultural moment—"Britney kissing Madonna!"—and it drew a lot of attention to both of us.

I got an idea for a collaboration while we were rehearsing for the VMAs. My crew and I were seated on silver metal folding chairs in the Culver City studio, discussing how the record company was lukewarm on my new song "Me Against the Music"—a tune I liked. I'd just done "I'm a Slave 4 U" on my previous record, and my label's owner, Barry Weiss, wanted more songs like that. But I was pushing for "Me Against the Music" with all my might.

"Then what if we do a feature on it?" I asked. Because of the incident that inspired it, a song can become a major hit. I reasoned that if we could find someone to sing on the tune, we could make a tale out of it.

"Who do you want to feature?" my boss said.

"Her!" I exclaimed, motioning across the room to Madonna. "Let's get her on the song."

"Holy shit," he exclaimed. "Yeah—that'd work." We agreed that instead of asking through her team, I would ask her directly.

So I went to see Madonna. "Let's talk," I suggested. I told her how much pleasure it would be to sing the song with her and how I thought we could help each other: it was something that would benefit both of us. She concurred.

"Me Against the Music" is still one of my favourite songs, and the collaboration with her is a big part of why.

On the first day of our two or three-day shoot for the song's video, we were told that a seam had come undone on Madonna's white suit and that a seamstress would be coming to mend it, causing a delay in our start time. I ended up having to sit in my trailer for hours while the suit was being repaired.

Really? I pondered. I had no idea taking so much time for myself was an option. I would never make production wait five minutes to fix a broken heel on my shoe. I'd do anything the director said, even if it meant hobbling into the scene without a heel or showing up barefoot.

Throughout our session, I was impressed by Madonna's refusal to compromise her vision. She kept the spotlight on herself. Collaboration with Madonna means going along with her ideas and being on her time for days. It was a big lesson for me, one that would take a long time to sink in: she sought authority, and she got it. She was the centre of attention because she made it a need for her to appear anywhere. She carved out that life for herself. I hoped I could do so while retaining the aspects of my nice-girl identity that I wanted to keep.

CHAPTER 5

MARRIED, RIGHT?

In the Zone, my new record, made me joyful. The album's first single, "Me Against the Music," featured Madonna. The following single was "Toxic," for which I received a Grammy Award. "Toxic" was both unique and hugely successful, and it remains one of my favourite songs to perform. To promote the album, I spent one night in New York City with an MTV camera crew filming a special called In the Zone & Out All Night. We drove all over town to perform at three different nightclubs: Show, Splash, and Avalon. It was thrilling to witness enormous crowds dancing to the new music. My supporters reminded me why I do what I do, as has happened numerous times during my career. But then there was a knock on my door one day. When I opened the door, four men walked right in, three of whom I didn't recognize. I'd never seen their expressions before. My father was the fourth.

They then sat me down on a sofa (the same one I still have in my bedroom). They immediately began bombarding me with questions, questions, and more questions. I was deafeningly silent, refusing to speak to anyone. I couldn't think of anything to say. A day later, I received a call from my team informing me that I would be speaking with Diane Sawyer... on the same sofa. Because of what had happened with Justin and everything I'd gone through, I felt as if I couldn't communicate with the rest of the world. I was traumatised and had a gloomy cloud over my head. I'd often gone to my apartment to be alone, but now I was being forced to speak to Diane Sawyer and cry in front of the entire country. It was utterly humiliating. I wasn't told what the questions would be ahead of time, and they were completely embarrassing. I was too fragile, too sensitive at the time, to conduct this type of interview. "He's going on television and saying you broke his heart," she inquired. You did something that caused him great distress. So much anguish. "What exactly did you do?"

I didn't want to reveal anything personal to the rest of the world. I didn't owe the media information about my breakup. I shouldn't have been compelled to speak on national television, to cry in front of a stranger, a woman who was constantly questioning me with hard question after harsh question. Instead, I felt exploited, set up in front of the entire world. That interview was a watershed moment for me—a switch had been flicked. Something black washed over my body. I felt myself transforming into a Bad Person, almost like a werewolf. I honestly believe that time in my life should have been spent growing rather than sharing everything with the world. It would have been the more effective method of healing. But I didn't have a choice. Nobody appeared to care about how I felt. We got back on the road. More buses are needed. More racks for costumes. Longer rehearsals. There will be more step-and-repeats. That was already one of the darkest periods of my life, and the tour's ambiance reflected that—a lot of steamy numbers, gloomy themes, and dreary lighting. My relationship with my brother, Bryan, also changed as a result of the tour. Bryan, who was now part of my team, was well compensated for the Onyx Hotel Tour, as was I. He also made a big deal with Elizabeth Arden for me. Nonetheless, I found it difficult not to resent him after I embarked on what was to be a really arduous tour while he stayed in Los Angeles and New York and lived his life. During those years, I lost contact with my brother. As a result, it felt as if I had lost Justin and Bryan at the same time. The tour was quite dismal. I damaged my knee terribly near the conclusion of the event in Moline, Illinois. I'd already injured my knee while practising for the music video for "Sometimes" from my debut album. That was more extreme: I'd sobbed uncontrollably. With this ailment, I only had to reschedule two dates, but I'd already begun to check out in my mind. I needed some lightness and joy in my life. Then Kevin Federline grabbed me. That's what I remember the most. We met in a club in Hollywood called Joseph's Café, where I used to sit at a table in the rear. There was an instant connection between us, from the moment I saw him—something that made me feel like I could escape everything that was difficult in my life. He held me—and I mean held me—in a pool for hours the first night we met. He was like that to me: stable, sturdy, and comforting. I recall going swimming with him and him just wrapping his arms around me in the water and not letting go until I told him to, no matter how long it took. It was more than just a sexual thing. It had nothing to do with passion. It was personal. He would hold me for as long as I desired. Has anyone in my life ever done something like that before? If so, I couldn't tell you when. Wasn't there anything better?

I hadn't been in a real relationship in a long time after what I'd gone through with J. Meanwhile, the press continued recommending notable guys for me to date—royalty, CEOs, and models. How could I explain that all I wanted was to be held by a man in a swimming pool for an hour?

I believe that many women, including myself, can be as strong as they want to be, to play this powerful role, but at the end of the day, after we've done our work, made our money, and taken care of everyone else, we want someone to hold us tight and tell us everything will be fine. I apologise. I realise it sounds regressive. But I believe it is a human instinct. We want to feel protected, alive, and sexy all at once. That's exactly what Kevin did for me. So I clutched him like there was no tomorrow. My friendship with Kevin was initially lighthearted. Kevin liked me exactly as I was. Being with a man who gave me permission to be exactly who I was seemed like such a gift after spending so much time trying to live up to society's standards. Kevin had a "bad boy" persona. Still, I had no idea he had a toddler or that his ex-girlfriend was eight months pregnant with his second child when we met. I had no idea. I was living in a cocoon, with few decent, close friends to whom I could trust and seek counsel. I had no idea until someone informed me, "You know he has a new baby, right?" after we'd been dating for a while.

I didn't believe it, but when I inquired, he confirmed it. He said he only saw them once a month.

"You have kids?" I said. "Do you have kids?" Not only one, but two children?"

So, obviously, something was done to me. I had absolutely no notion.

Even though I was miserable, I had to return to work in the spring of 2004 to meet my contractual obligations. I reasoned that it would be acceptable if Kevin could accompany me, and he agreed to attend. We had so much fun on that tour; he kept me distracted from the work, which felt as difficult as it had ever been. I didn't have to return to my hotel room alone after the shows. We were talking on the plane back home, and I asked him to marry me. He said no, then proposed. We collaborated on tour diaries. The original plan was to do a documentary similar to Madonna's Truth or Dare, but it turned out to be more of a collection of our home movies, especially after I got hurt again, and it was later broadcast as a reality program called Britney and Kevin: Chaotic. The Onyx Hotel Tour was simply awful. For starters, it was far too sexual. Justin had publicly humiliated me, so my onstage retort had to go there as well. But it was really dreadful. I despised it at the time. In fact, I was so sick of that awful trip that I prayed every night. "God, just break my arm," I said. Make my leg snap. "Can you break something?" Then, on June 8, 2004, with two months of concerts left, I fell again on the set of my video for "Outrageous," inflicting another knee damage and requiring surgery. The remaining tour dates were cancelled. I remembered how much I'd struggled as a youngster while undergoing physical treatment for my knee. The ordeal had been agonising. Even though my legs were giving me excruciating pain, I had to move them up and down. As a result, when the physicians offered me Vicodin, I accepted it. I didn't want to go through that ordeal again. I just went to my Manhattan apartment, climbed into my princess bed, and told everybody who wanted to talk to me—friends, family, businesspeople—to "Leave me alone." No, I'm not interested in doing anything or seeing anyone." And I didn't want to go back on tour for a long time if I could avoid it. Part of it was because I felt I had earned the right to make my own personal decisions after such a demanding schedule. I felt duped into returning to work immediately after my breakup with Justin since it was all I knew. The Onyx tour was a blunder. But I kept telling myself that I should simply do what I was meant to do, which was work. I now see that I should have sat back and taken my time getting over Justin's split before resuming touring. The music industry is simply too harsh and cruel. You frequently go to a different city every day. There isn't any consistency. When you're on the road, it's impossible to find peace. When I made Britney Spears: Live and More! video special in Hawaii in 2000, I saw how simple TV can be. Touring is not a luxury in the business; television is.

My sister had also recently secured a lucrative Nickelodeon contract. I was delighted for her. Seeing her practise her lines and do wardrobe fittings made me wish I had a profession that was more like the pleasant world of children's television. I liked recalling the Mickey Mouse Club and how simple everything looked back then. I expected Kevin to provide me with the stability I desired, as well as the independence I desired. Many folks were disappointed in Kevin and me. Whether I wanted it or not, I was one of the world's biggest stars at the time. He was leading a more quiet existence. I had to defend our friendship in front of everyone. That October, Kevin and I married. We had a "surprise" ceremony in September, but the lawyers required extra time to work on the prenup, so the legal event was postponed for a few weeks. The ceremony was videotaped. The bridesmaids wore burgundy and I wore a strapless gown. After the ceremony, I changed into a pink sweatsuit with the words MRS. FEDERLINE, and everyone else changed into Juicy tracksuits as well, because we were going to a club to dance all night. Now that I was married and contemplating having children, I decided to start saying no to things that didn't feel right, such as the Onyx tour. My bosses and I had a falling out. On my website, I sent a letter to followers in which I announced that I would be taking some time off to enjoy my life.

"I've actually learned to say 'NO!'" I wrote with sincerity. "With this newfound independence, it's as if people aren't sure how to act around me... I apologise for making my life seem chaotic over the last two years. It's most likely because IT WAS! I now understand what they mean when they speak of child stars. Going and going and going has been all I've known since I was fifteen... Please keep in mind that the times are changing, and so am I."

I felt so much better after declaring my determination to finally take control of my own life. Everything is about to change around here! I thought exuberantly. Then they did it.

Two facts regarding pregnancy: I enjoyed both sex and food. Both of those items were absolutely wonderful with both of my pregnancies. Aside from that, I can't say there was anything that made me happy. I was simply being cruel. You didn't want to hear from me for two years. I hardly wanted to be around anyone. I was venomous. I didn't want anyone around me, not even my mother. I was a true mother bear. America's sweetheart and the world's meanest woman. I was also protective of Jamie Lynn. I arrived on the set to confront the actress after she complained to me about a co-star on her TV show. "Are you spreading rumours about my sister?" I must have looked enormously pregnant and ranting at a teenage (and, I later learned, innocent) girl. (I apologise to that young actress.)

When I was pregnant, I told everyone to back off: "Stand back!" There's a baby in the house!

It's true what they say: no one can prepare you for having a baby. It's nothing short of miraculous. You're constructing a new body. You grow up saying, "That person's pregnant." "That person had a baby." But when you actually go through it, it's overwhelming. It was a spiritual experience, with an immensely strong link. My mother had often mentioned how terrible childbirth could be. She never let me forget that she'd been in terrible labour with me for many hours. Everyone is unique, after all. Some ladies have it easier than others. I was frightened about having a natural birth. When the doctor suggested a C-section, I declined. I was overjoyed. On September 14, 2005, Sean Preston was born. You could tell he was a sweet, caring little boy right away.

Three months later, I became pregnant again. I was overjoyed to have two kids so close in age. Still, it was difficult for my body, and I felt a lot of sadness and loneliness at the time. I felt like the entire universe was conspiring against me. The primary hazard I had to watch out for was paparazzi assault. If I stayed out of the spotlight, the cameras would definitely leave me alone, I reasoned. Photographers tracked me down whether I was at home or attempting to go to the store. They were there every day and night, waiting for me to come out. Nobody in the media appeared to notice that I was already harsh on myself. I might be crazy, but I was always a people-pleaser at heart. Even when I was at my lowest, I cared what other people thought of me. I grew up in the South, where manners are highly valued. To this day, regardless of their age, I address men as "sir" and ladies as "ma'am." Just on the level of etiquette, it was excruciating to be treated with such contempt—with loathing. I documented everything I did with the babies. When I drove away from the paparazzi with Sean Preston on my lap, it was interpreted as proof that I was unfit. I was cornered by paparazzi with him at the Malibu Country Mart as well—they kept taking my picture while I held him and cried. I was surrounded by photographers as I attempted to exit a building and into a car in New York, pregnant with Jayden James and carrying Sean Preston. I was told I had to enter the car on the other side, so I said, "Oh," and made my way through a thousand camera shutters and yells of "Britney! Britney!" to get in.

If you watch the movie rather than just the still photographs, you'll notice that while carrying a cup of water in one hand and my kid in the other, my heel rotated and I almost fell—but I didn't. And in catching myself, I didn't drop the water or the baby, who, by the way, was unfazed.

"This is why I need a gun," I told the camera, which probably didn't go down well. But I was at a loss for words. The mags seemed to want nothing more than a shot with the title "Britney Spears got HUGE!" She's not even wearing makeup!" As if those two things were a sin—as if gaining weight was something cruel I'd done to them, a betrayal. When did I decide to stay seventeen for the rest of my life?

Kevin began working harder on his own songs when Sean Preston was a baby. He wanted to make his own name, which I encouraged him to do. He was recording a lot because it was his passion. I'd occasionally swing by a studio where he was working, and it felt like a clubhouse. I could smell the marijuana wafting out the studio door before I even entered. He and the other guys would go high, and I felt like I was in their way. I wasn't invited to their celebration. I couldn't handle being near marijuana smoke. Even the fragrance made me sick. And I had the baby and was pregnant, so I couldn't just stay out all day. So I generally stayed at home. It's not like it was a huge deal. I had a lovely house—a dream house. We would hire a fantastic chef—too pricey to use on a regular basis. But, while eating something prepared by the chef, I exclaimed, "Oh my God, this is the most delicious thing I've ever had, and can you just live with us?" "I absolutely adore you!" And I meant it when I said I loved him. I was happy for any extra assistance around the house. Maybe this is how married couples are, I thought as Kevin and I drew more apart. You alternate allowing each other to be a little selfish. This is his first taste of celebrity. I should give it to him.

I told myself, "He's my husband." I'm expected to appreciate him and accept him on a deeper level than I would accept a new boyfriend. He is the father of my children. His demeanour is different now, but it could change again. People say he'll break up with me when I'm pregnant, as he did with the mother of his first two children when they were infants, but no way! He will not be the same as he was with his other family. I was lying to myself by making up all these justifications in my head—I was completely in denial that he was leaving me. I took a plane to New York to visit him. He'd been so disconnected that I felt we needed to spend some time together as a family. I checked into a luxury hotel in the city, eager to see my spouse. But he didn't notice me. He seemed to want to pretend I didn't exist. His manager, who had been on my team for years, also refused to see me. He was now on Kevin's team, and it appeared that they were done with me.

"Damn, really?" I said.

All I could think about was getting near enough to Kevin to ask him what was going on. "When you left to come out here, we hugged," I wanted to add. You kissed me on the lips. What exactly is going on? "What occurred?"

I had a feeling something was wrong, that he was changing, especially once he began getting press and feeling himself. He once arrived home late and said he'd been to a party. He exclaimed, "Justin Timberlake was there!" "Lindsay Lohan was, too!"

Do you think I'm interested in your ridiculous party? I pondered. Do you have any idea how many such events I've attended? Some of those people I've known longer than you. Do you realise how much I went through with Justin? No, you have no idea. I didn't say any of it, but I wanted to say it all and more. Kevin was completely fascinated by celebrity and power. I've seen celebrities and money wreck individuals before, and I saw it happen to Kevin in slow motion. In my experience, when most people, particularly guys, receive that kind of attention, it's all over. They are obsessed with it. And it's bad for them. Some celebrities manage their celebrity successfully. They have a point of view. They enjoy being admired, but not too much. They understand who to listen to and who to disregard. Receiving accolades and prizes is exciting, and being a star for the first two years is an unforgettable experience. Some people, in my opinion, are born to be famous. I'm not. It was alright for the first two or three years, but what about my true self? I used to play basketball in school. I didn't cheerlead because I didn't want to be out there. I was on the field. That was my favourite part. But what about fame? That world does not exist, my friends. It's not true. You agree since, of course, it will pay the family's bills and everything. However, it lacked the sense of genuine life in my opinion. That's probably why I had my children. So you're receiving prizes and fame? I really enjoyed it. But it's not going to last for me. I enjoy sweating on the floor during rehearsals or simply playing ball and making a shot. I enjoy the work. I enjoy practising. That is more genuine and valuable than anything else. I honestly envy people who can make celebrities work for them, because I avoid it. I get extremely shy. Jennifer Lopez, for example, struck me from the start as someone who was extremely excellent at being famous—in indulging people's interest in her while also knowing where to draw the line. She was usually well-mannered. She carried herself with dignity at all times. Kevin had no idea how to do any of that. I'll admit that I'm not very good at it either. I'm a worrisome individual. I've grown to avoid most forms of attention as I've gotten older, possibly because I've been injured in the past. I should have known my marriage was over at the time of that harrowing journey to New York, but I still felt it might be saved. Kevin thereafter went on to another studio, this time in Las Vegas. So I went there, intending to speak with him.

He had his head shaved when I found him. He was getting ready to shoot the album cover. He was constantly in the studio. He truly believed he was a rapper at this point. Bless his heart—he did take it very seriously. So I arrived in Vegas with Sean Preston, still pregnant with Jayden James, and full of sympathy for Kevin's predicament. Everyone seemed to be doubting him as he tried to make things happen for himself. That was something I was familiar with. It's nerve-racking to put yourself out there like that. You must truly believe in yourself, even when the world makes you doubt your abilities. But I also felt he should have checked in more frequently and spent more time with me. My heart belonged to our small family. I'd been carrying his children for a long time and had made many sacrifices. I had almost given up on my job. I'd done everything I could to make our lives feasible. I dropped Sean Preston off at the hotel with a nanny and arrived at the video set. I was told yet again that he did not want to see me. He has later stated that this is not true and that he would never have done such a thing. All I remember is what happened: security officers who had previously worked at my house stood at the entrance and refused to let me in. Everyone on that set seemed to be avoiding me.

I spotted a group of young folks partying through a window. The stage had been transformed into a nightclub. Kevin and the other actors were smoking marijuana and smiling. I felt entirely detached from myself. I stood there watching the action for a while, not wanting anyone inside to notice. Then I said to the security guard, "Okay, great," turned around, and returned to the hotel.

I was at the hotel, distraught, when the doorbell rang.

Jason Trawick, one of my brother's old buddies, called when I answered. He was aware of what had occurred.

He said, "How are you doing?" He appeared really interested in how I responded.

I pondered the last time someone asked me that.

CHAPTER 6

A MOTHER

Jayden James was born on September 12, 2006, just before Sean Preston's first birthday. From the moment he was born, he was a cheerful child. I felt so light after I'd had both sons, almost like I was a bird or a feather, like I could glide away. My body felt amazing to me. Is this what being a thirteen-year-old feels like again? I pondered. I no longer had a stomach.

"Wow, you look so skinny!" exclaimed one of my pals.

"Well, I've been pregnant for two years straight," she replied.

I felt like an entirely different person after the babies. It was perplexing. On the one hand, I found myself unexpectedly fitting back into my clothes. When I tried them on, they looked great! It was a revelation to rediscover my love for clothes. I said, "Holy sh*t!" My entire body! On the other hand, I'd been so relieved to know that these babies were safe inside of me. When I couldn't keep them secure inside my body anymore, I became depressed. They appeared so defenceless in the world of squabbling paparazzi and tabloids. I wanted them back inside me, away from the rest of the world.

One headline asked, "Why is Britney so camera-shy with Jayden?"

After Jayden was born, Kevin and I had gotten so good at hiding the kids that many were puzzled why no images of him had been released. I believe that if anyone had given the question a second consideration, they could have made some educated guesses. However, no one was actually asking the question. They just continued acting as if I owed it to them to let the men who were always attempting to catch me looking fat snap pictures of my infant sons. One of the first things I had to do after each birth was count the number of enemy combatants in the parking lot. Every time I checked, they seemed to multiply. There were constantly more cars than appeared to be safe. Seeing so many men gathered to photograph my children made my blood run cold. With a lot of money on the line in photo rights, it was their duty to capture images of the guys at any cost. And my boys were so small. It was my responsibility to keep them secure. I was concerned that the flashing lights and shouts would startle them. Kevin and I had to create techniques to cover them with blankets while still allowing them to breathe. I couldn't even do it without a blanket.

I wasn't interested in conducting publicity that year, although I did do one interview for Dateline with Matt Lauer. People were asking him about me, he added, including "Is Britney a bad mom?" He never stated who was questioning them. Everyone, it appears. And he inquired as to what I believed it would take for the paparazzi to leave me alone. I wished he'd asked them so that whatever it was, I could do it. Fortunately, my house was a secure haven. Our marriage was in turmoil, but Kevin and I had constructed an amazing mansion in Los Angeles, right next door to Mel Gibson's. Sandy from Grease also lived close. When I saw her, I'd say, "Hi, Olivia Newton-John! Olivia Newton-John, how are you?"

It was a dream home for us. The pool was accessible by a slide. There was a sandbox with toys for the youngsters to build sandcastles in. We had a tiny playhouse with steps and a ladder, as well as a tiny porch. And we just kept building on it. I didn't like the wooden floors, so I replaced them with marble—of course, white marble. The interior designer was adamantly opposed. He went on to say, "Marble floors are super slippery and hard if you fall down."

"I want marble!" I yelled. "I need marble."

It was both my house and my nest. It was just stunning. But I guess I realised then that I'd turned strange.

I'd had these two children consecutively. My hormones were out of control. I was cruel as heck and extremely dictatorial. Having children was a huge thing for me. I had gone beyond in my efforts to make our home perfect. Now that I think about it, that was terrible. Please accept my apologies, contractors. I believe I was overly concerned. I hired a muralist to create imaginative images of small boys on the moon for the boys' rooms. I simply went all out. It had always been my desire to have children and raise them in the most comfortable setting I could devise. They were wonderful, lovely, and everything I'd ever desired. I wanted to give them the entire solar system. When I refused to let my mother hold Jayden for the first two months, I began to suspect that I was being overprotective. Even after that, I'd only let her hold him for five minutes. I needed him back in my arms. That is excessive. That I now understand. I should not have been so commanding.

Again, I believe what happened when I first saw them after they were born was similar to what happened to me after Justin's breakup: it was the Benjamin Button effect. I went back in time. As a new mother, I felt as if a piece of me had become a baby. One part of me was a demanding adult shrieking about white marble, while another part of me became quite childlike.

Those first few months after Jayden returned home flew by. I bought a dog. Felicia came and went in and out of my life. I'd coloured my hair black while pregnant with Jayden. In an attempt to make it blond again, I dyed it purple. I had to visit a beauty parlour to have my hair fully stripped and dyed a realistic shade of brown. It took an eternity to get it right. Almost everything in my life seemed that way. To say the least, there was a lot of upheaval: the breakup with J and the arduous Onyx tour, marrying someone no one thought was a good match, and then attempting to be a decent mother inside of a marriage that was failing in real time. Despite this, I was always joyful and creative in the studio. I felt very liberated when recording for Blackout. I got to play since I was working with incredible producers. Nate Hills, who recorded under the name Danja, was more into dance and EDM than pop; he exposed me to new sounds and allowed me to expand my vocal range in new directions. I liked that no one was overthinking things and that I was able to express what I liked and disliked. I understood exactly what I wanted, and I loved a lot of what was presented to me. It was exciting to get into the studio and hear these beautiful sounds and then record a vocal over them. Despite my reputation at the time, I arrived determined and eager to work. What was going on outside the studio was the most upsetting. The paparazzi were like a zombie army, attempting to get in at every opportunity. They attempted to scale the walls and snap photographs through the windows. Attempting to enter and depart a building felt like a military operation. It was frightening.

Teresa LaBarbera Whites, my A&R rep who was also a mother, did everything she could to assist. She installed a baby swing in one of our studios, which I thought was a very thoughtful gift.

The album served as a sort of rallying call. After years of being precise in order to impress my mother and father, it was time to say "Fuck you." I stopped doing business the way I had always done it. I began filming footage on the street alone. I'd go into pubs with a friend who'd just bring a camera, and that's how we shot "Gimme More."

To be clear, I'm not bragging about it. "Gimme More" is by far the worst video I've ever created. I despise it because it is so tacky. It appears that we spent only three thousand dollars to shoot it. Nonetheless, despite its flaws, it served its purpose. And the more I went and did things for myself, the more intriguing people began to notice and want to work with me. By word of mouth, I ended up meeting some pretty nice folks at random. Blackout was one of the simplest and most rewarding albums I've ever made. It came together quite quickly. I'd walk into the studio, stay for thirty minutes, and then go. That wasn't on purpose; it had to be quick. If I stayed in one spot for too long, the photographers outside would multiply like Pac-Man being pursued by ghosts. My survival strategy was to get in and out of studios as quickly as possible. When I was recording "Hot as Ice," When I arrived into the studio, there were six huge males sitting there with me. Being with all those gentlemen quietly listening to me sing was perhaps one of the most spiritual recording experiences of my life. My voice rose to its greatest pitch. I sang it again and then departed. I didn't have to even attempt. Even though making Blackout felt amazing, life was still staring at me from all sides. Everything was so severe from one minute to the next. I needed more self-worth and value than I could muster at the time. Even though it was a difficult time in almost every other way, it was fantastic artistically. Something about my mental state made me a better artist.

Making the Blackout record gave me a rush. I had the opportunity to work in the best studios. It was an exciting time.

Unfortunately, when family life is poor, it takes over and makes everything else feel better. I lament how bad things got with my family, but I'm still quite proud of that CD. Many musicians have stated that it affected them, and many fans have stated that it is their favourite.

Meanwhile, Kevin was getting a lot of coverage, as if he'd just hit a grand slam in the World Series. I had forgotten who he was. Then he was approached to appear in a Nationwide Super Bowl commercial. It didn't matter that the ad featured him making fun of himself as a fast-food worker who aspires to be a celebrity. I never saw him again after he accepted that deal. It was as if he was too good to talk to me. He told everyone that becoming a father meant everything to him, that it was the best thing in his life. You'd never guess. Because, unfortunately, he was away a lot.

CHAPTER 7

END THE MARRIAGE

I gave it my all when I married Kevin. Look into my wedding pics to see how much I was in love and ready to start a new chapter in my life. I wished to have children with this man. I wished for a cosy home. I wished I could grow old with him.

If I did not file for divorce, Kevin, according to my lawyer, would. From this, I deduced that Kevin wanted to file for divorce but felt terrible about it. He realised that filing would make him look better in public. Kevin was going to file for divorce anyhow, according to my lawyer. I was told that doing it first would save me from shame. I didn't want to be embarrassed, so I turned in the papers in early November 2006, when Jayden was only two months old. Kevin and I both asked for sole custody of the boys. What I didn't anticipate was Kevin's demand that I pay his legal bills. And, because I had formally initiated the divorce, I would be held publicly responsible for the dissolution of my young family.

The media coverage was out of this world. It was probably perfect for Kevin's CD, which came out a week before we divorced, but I got slammed. Some people attempted to be sympathetic, but in the press, they regularly criticised Kevin, which wasn't very helpful.

Later that month, I delivered a speech at the American Music Awards. While I waited to go onstage, Jimmy Kimmel delivered a monologue and a spoof about Kevin, whom he dubbed "the world's first-ever no-hit wonder." They transported a stand-in in a crate onto a truck and dumped it in the water. This, on the other hand, was the father of my two infant sons. The violence directed at him bothered me. The entire audience erupted in laughter. It caught me off guard because I had no idea it was going to happen. I walked onstage and handed the award to Mary J. Blige, but then I went backstage and tried to hide the fact that I was surprised and didn't appreciate it. I also didn't think that treating my ex-husband that way would benefit me throughout a custody battle. Except for me, everyone seemed thrilled with the news of our divorce. I had no urge to rejoice. In retrospect, Justin and Kevin were both quite wise. They understood exactly what they were doing, and I was there beside them. That is the problem with this business. I didn't know how to play the game. I had no idea how to express myself on any level. I used to be a terrible dresser, and I'll admit, I still am. And I'm working on it right now. I will try. But, as much as I admit my flaws, I know I am a good person. I understand now that you had to be smart, brutal, and deliberate to play the game, which I had no idea what it was. I was completely innocent—only oblivious. I was a recently divorced mother of two tiny boys with no time to straighten my hair before entering a sea of photographers. So I was young and made a lot of mistakes. But I'll say this: I wasn't lying. I was simply inept.

Justin and Kevin completely destroyed one piece of my personality. I used to believe in people. But, following my divorce and separation from Justin, I never trusted anyone again.

Paris Hilton was one of the sweetest individuals to me when I really needed it. Much of America rejected her as a party girl, but I thought she was elegant—the way she stood on the red carpet and always had an arched eyebrow when someone said something negative about her. She noticed that I had babies and was going through a breakup, and I believe she felt sorry for me. She came over to my house and was quite helpful. She was quite sweet to me. Aside from that night in Vegas with Jason Trawick, no one had been so lovely to me in a long time. We began to hang out. For the first time in a long time, she urged me to attempt to have fun. I went through my party stage with Paris. But, to be clear, it was never as wild as the media made it out to be. I used to spend hardly any time outside. Finally, when I left home for a few hours with the kids properly supervised at home by qualified caregivers, remained out late, and drank like any other twentysomething, I heard nothing but that I was the worst mother who'd ever lived and a terrible person. The headlines were rife with accusations: She's a slacker! She's high on drugs!

I never had an alcohol issue. I enjoyed drinking, but it was never out of hand. Do you want to know what my go-to medicine is? Apart from drinking, what else did I do? Adderall is an amphetamine that is prescribed to children for ADHD. Yes, Adderall got me high, but what I found far more enticing was that it made me feel less depressed for a few hours. It was the only drug that worked for me as an antidepressant, and I desperately needed one. I've never been interested in hard drugs. I saw lots of musicians performing all of that, but it wasn't for me. Where I grew up, we drank beer more than anything else; to this day, I avoid drinking costly wine because it hurts my throat. And, other than that one time in New York when I injured my heel, I've never enjoyed cannabis. It makes me feel stupid and foolish if I only get a high contact from being around it. It irritates me.

Do you know what Paris and I did on that purportedly insane night with Lindsay Lohan that everyone made such a big deal about? We got wasted. That's all! We were vacationing at a beach home, and my mother was watching the children, so I went out with Paris. We were high, drinking and acting crazy. It felt fantastic to hang out with friends and be free. There wasn't a single thing wrong with it.

I walked inside the beach house at the end of one night, satisfied with my excursion but still a touch tipsy. My mother was waiting for me. She screamed at me when I stepped in, and we got into a huge fight.

She said it was due to my inebriation. She wasn't mistaken. I certainly was. But that wasn't a violation of some unwritten norm in our household. And I'd had her babysit that night so I could go out responsibly without the kids witnessing their mother under the influence. My heart was killed by the embarrassment I felt. Okay, I thought as I stood there reeling. I guess it's illegal for me to party. My mother was continually making me feel awful or guilty of something, even though I had worked so hard to be decent. That's how my family has always treated me: as if I were bad. The fight was a watershed moment in my relationship with my mother. I couldn't go back to how things were before. We tried, but it didn't work out. My parents never appeared to think I was worth anything, no matter how many followers I had throughout the world. How could you treat your child this way while she was going through a divorce, lonely and lost? Giving someone no grace during a difficult moment is simply not nice, especially when you can't take as well as you give. They didn't like it when I started to speak up and throw it back at them a little—God knows they weren't perfect. But they still had a strong emotional hold on me.

CHAPTER 8

MY BOYS

For me, everything everyone says about being a mom was true. My boys give meaning to my life. I was quite aback by how much genuine and immediate affection I felt for those small beings. However, being a mother while under so much pressure at home and in the world was far more difficult than I had anticipated. I began to act strange after being cut off from my buddies. I know you're meant to focus solely on being a mother during those times, but it was difficult for me to sit down and play with them every day, to prioritise being a mother. I was completely perplexed. Everything I'd known my entire life was being revealed on every level. I had no idea where to go or what to do. Was I supposed to go home to Louisiana, build a wall around my house, and hide? What I can see now but couldn't see then is that every aspect of normal life had been taken away from me, including going out in public without becoming a headline, making typical mistakes as a new mother of two babies, and feeling like I could trust the people around me. I had neither freedom nor security. I was also suffering from severe postpartum depression, as I now know. I'll admit that I felt I couldn't live if things didn't improve. Everyone else was going about their business, but I was being observed from every angle. No one said anything to Justin and Kevin while they had all the sex and smoked all the pot in the world. When I got home following a night at the clubs, my mother ripped into me. It scared me to do anything. My family rendered me immobile. I was drawn to anyone who would step in and act as a buffer between me and them, especially those who would take me out to party and divert me from all the surveillance I was subjected to. In the long term, not all of these people were excellent, but at the time I was desperate for anyone who seemed to want to help me in any way and who seemed to have the capacity to keep my parents at bay.

Kevin attempted to persuade everyone that I was utterly out of control as part of his effort for full custody. He began to suggest that I should not have my children at all.

When he stated that, I thought to myself, "Surely this is a joke." This is strictly for the tabloids. When you hear about married celebrities quarrelling, you never know what's true. I usually assume that a lot of what you hear is a ruse to obtain the upper hand in a custody dispute by feeding things to the papers. So I waited for him to return the boys to me once he had taken them. He not only refused to return them to me, but he also refused to allow me to see them for weeks on end.

Sandra, my aunt, died in January 2007 after a long and arduous battle with ovarian cancer. She was like a second mother to me. At the burial, I cried harder than I ever had before over Aunt Sandra's grave. Working seemed impossible to me. During that time, a well-known director called me about a movie he was working on. "I have a role for you to play," he explained. "It's a really dark role." I declined because I believed it would be detrimental to my emotional health. But I wonder if simply knowing the part made me instinctively go there in my thoughts and envision what it would be like to be her. I'd been feeling a veil of darkness on the inside for a long time. On the outside, though, I'd attempted to keep looking and acting the way others expected me to—sweet and attractive all the time. But the sheen had worn away to the point that there was nothing left. I was like a raw nerve.

I went to beg to see the boys in February, after not seeing them for weeks and weeks, absolutely overcome with grief. Kevin refused to let me in. I pleaded with him. Sean Preston was seventeen months old and Jayden James was five months old. I pictured them wondering why their mother didn't want to be with them because they didn't know where she was. I intended to attack them with a battering ram. I had no idea what to do. The paparazzi were present throughout. I can't put into words how humiliated I felt. I was surrounded. I was out and about, being pursued by these men who were waiting for me to do anything they could photograph. So I provided them with some material that night. I went to a hair salon and shaved off all of my hair with clippers. It was hilarious to everyone. Look how insane she is! My parents were also humiliated by me. Nobody seemed to grasp that I was just insane with grief. My children had been abducted from me. Everyone, including my mother, was terrified of me with my head shaved. No one would talk to me because I was too unattractive. I was aware that my long hair was a large part of what people appreciated about me. I was aware that many men believed long hair was attractive. Shaving my head was my way of telling the world, "Fuck you!" You want me to look nice for you? You're a jerk. You expect me to be good to you? You're a jerk. Do you want me to be your fantasy girl? You're a jerk. For years, I'd been a good girl. I'd smiled politely as TV show hosts mocked my breasts, while American parents said I was destroying their children by wearing a crop top, while executives patted my hand condescendingly and questioned my career choices despite selling millions of records, and while my family acted like I was evil. And I was fed up with it. I didn't care at the end of the day. All I wanted was to see my boys. It made me sick to think about the hours, days, and weeks I spent away from them. My favourite memories are of taking naps with my children. Taking naps with my lovely infants, smelling their hair, holding their little hands—that's the closest I've ever felt to God.

I grew quite enraged. I believe many other ladies feel the same way "If someone took my baby away from me, I would have done a lot more than get a haircut," a buddy of mine once commented. "I would have set fire to the city."

I lost it over and over again over those weeks without my children. I didn't even know how to look after myself. I'd had to leave the house I loved due to the divorce and was now living in a strange English-style cottage in Beverly Hills. The paparazzi were buzzing around like sharks when there's blood in the sea. It seemed almost sacred when I initially shaved my head. I was living on a pure being level. For when I needed to go out into the world, I ordered seven short bob wigs. But I didn't want to see anyone if I couldn't see my sons. My cousin Alli drove me back to Kevin's a few days after I shaved my head. At the very least, I expected no paparazzi to be present this time. However, one of the photographers was reportedly tipped off, and he contacted his pal. They came looking for me when we stopped at a gas station. They kept snapping flash photos with a large camera and videotaping me through the window while I sat in the passenger seat, devastated, waiting for Alli to return. "How are you doing?," one of them inquired. How are you doing? "I'm worried about you."

We continued on to Kevin's. The two paparazzi continued to follow us, capturing pictures as I was denied admittance to Kevin's once more. I turned away, hoping to get a glimpse of my own children. Alli pulled over after we departed so we could figure out what to do next. The videographer had returned to my window.

"What I'm going to do, Britney—all I'm going to do—is ask you a few questions," one of them remarked, a cruel expression on his face. He didn't ask if he could. He was preparing to do something for me. "And then I'm going to leave you alone."

Alli began pleading with the men to leave her alone. "Please, gentlemen. Guys, don't do it. "Please, please..."

She was so courteous, and she was appealing with them as if she was begging them to save our lives, which she was. But they wouldn't give up. I yelled.They liked it when I reacted. One man refused to go until he got his way. He kept smirking and asking me the same horrible questions over and over, hoping I'd react again. His voice was filled with harshness and a lack of humanity. This was one of the darkest times in my life, and he pursued me. Couldn't he just treat me like a human? Could he not back down? But he refused. He simply kept coming. He kept asking me how I felt about not being able to see my children. He was beaming. I finally snapped. I jumped out of the car with the only thing I could reach, a green umbrella. I wasn't going to punch him because, even in my worst moments, I'm not that type of guy. I smashed into the next nearest item, which happened to be his automobile. Really, it's pathetic. A raincoat. You can't even hurt yourself with an umbrella. A desperate person made a desperate move. I was so embarrassed by what I'd done that I wrote an apology email to the photo agency, noting that I'd been considered for a dark film role, which was true, and that I wasn't quite myself, which was also true. Later, in an interview for a documentary about me, that paparazzo would observe, "That was not a good night for her... But it was a terrific night for us since we got the game-winning shot."

My husband, Hesam, now informs me that shaved heads are a thing for beautiful girls. It's a mood, he adds, a decision not to conform to conventional beauty standards. He tries to help me feel better about it because he is saddened by how much it still bothers me.

I felt as if I were living on the precipice of a cliff. I went to Bryan's residence in Los Angeles after shaving my head. He was accompanied by two women from his past in Mississippi, as well as my mother. My mother didn't even look at me since I was so unattractive. It just demonstrated that the world is primarily concerned about your physical look, even if you are in pain and at your lowest point.

I'd been informed that going to rehab would help me regain custody that winter. So, despite the fact that I believed I had a fury and grief problem rather than a substance misuse problem, I went. My father was present when I arrived. He sat across from me, with three picnic tables in between. He told her, "You are a disgrace."

When I reflect back, I wonder why I didn't call Big Rob for assistance. I was already ashamed and embarrassed, and now my father was calling me a disgrace. It was the epitome of flogging a dead horse. He was treating me like a dog, a very nasty dog. I had no one. I felt completely alone. One advantage of rehab was that I began the healing process. I was adamant about making the best of a bad circumstance. When I was released, I was able to obtain interim joint custody through the assistance of an excellent attorney. But the battle with Kevin raged on, and it was eating me alive.

Blackout, the project I'm most pleased of in my entire career, was released right around Halloween in 2007. I was supposed to perform "Gimme More" at the Video Music Awards to help promote it. I didn't want to, but my team was putting pressure on me to go out there and prove to the world that I was fine. The only difficulty with this strategy was that I wasn't feeling well. Nothing was going right backstage at the VMAs that night. My costume and hair extensions were both malfunctioning. I hadn't gotten any sleep the night before. I felt woozy. It had been less than a year since I'd delivered my second child in two years, yet everyone was making fun of my lack of six-pack abs. I couldn't believe I had to go up onstage feeling the way I did.

Backstage, I ran into Justin. I hadn't seen him in a long time. Everything was going swimmingly in his world. He was at the top of his game in every manner, and he exuded confidence. I was experiencing a panic attack. I hadn't practised enough. I despised the way I looked. I could tell it was going to be horrible. I went out there and did my best at the time, which was, admittedly, far from my best at other times. While performing, I could see myself on camera throughout the auditorium; it was like staring in a fun-house mirror. I'm not going to justify or say that the performance was wonderful, but as performers, we all have bad nights. They don't normally have such severe repercussions. You also don't normally experience one of your worst days in the same place and time as your ex has one of his best. Justin began his performance by gliding down the runway. He was flirting with girls in the audience, including one who spun around and arched her back as he sang to her, shaking her breasts. Then he was on stage with Nelly Furtado and Timbaland, having so much fun, being so free, and being so light. Sarah Silverman, a comedian, came on stage later that night to roast me. She stated that by the age of twenty-five, I'd accomplished everything worthwhile in my life. She referred to my two children as "the most adorable mistakes you'll ever see." But I didn't find out about it till later. Backstage, I was sobbing uncontrollably. The newspapers mocked my body and my performance in the days and weeks that followed.

Dr. Phil described it as a train wreck. When Blackout was released in October 2007, the only press I did was a live radio interview with Ryan Seacrest. During the interview, Ryan Seacrest asked me questions such as, "How do you respond to those who criticise you as a mom?" and "Do you feel like you're doing everything you can for your kids?" with the question "How often will you see them?"

It seemed like that was all everybody wanted to speak about: whether or not I was a fit mother. Not about how I'd created such a powerful record while carrying two babies on my hips and being pursued by dozens of dangerous men every day. My management team resigned. As a witness in the custody dispute, a bodyguard appeared in court with Gloria Allred by his side. He said I was using narcotics, but he was not cross-examined. A parenting coach assigned by the court stated that I adored my children and that we were definitely attached. She also stated that there was nothing in my home that could be classified as abuse. But that didn't make the news. I had the boys one day in early January 2008, and at the end of the visit, a security guard who used to work for me but now worked for Kevin arrived to bring them up. First, he loaded Preston into the car. When he arrived to pick up Jayden, I realised I might never see my boys again. Given the state of my custody case, I was frightened that if I returned the children, I wouldn't see them again. I dashed into the bathroom with Jayden and locked the door—I couldn't bear the thought of him leaving. I didn't want anyone to take my child. A friend arrived at the bathroom door and informed me that the security guy would wait. I sobbed as I held Jayden. But no one was willing to give me more time. Before I knew it, a SWAT team in black suits pushed through the restroom door, as if I'd done something wrong. The only thing I was guilty of was being anxious to keep my own children for a few more hours and to receive some assurance that I wouldn't lose them permanently. I just glanced at my pal and said, "But you said he'd wait..."

After they had Jayden, they handcuffed me to a gurney and drove me to the hospital. The hospital released me before the 72-hour hold was up. However, the harm had already been done. It didn't help that the paparazzi were becoming more aggressive in their pursuit of me. A fresh custody court was convened, and I was told that because I'd panicked because I was afraid of losing the kids, I'd be permitted to see them even less. Nobody seemed to have my back. Even my relatives appeared unconcerned. I learned of my sixteen-year-old sister's pregnancy from a tabloid exclusive over the holidays. It had been hidden from me by my family. This was around the time Jamie Lynn was on the verge of filing for emancipation from our parents. Taking away her cell phone is one of the things she has accused them of. She was forced to communicate with the outside world using burner phones that she kept hidden. I now understand that if someone isn't doing well—and I wasn't doing well—that's the moment to come to that person and hold them. Kevin took away my entire universe. He sucked the life out of me. And neither did my relatives. I began to suspect that they were secretly applauding the fact that I was going through the worst period of my life. But that couldn't be right, could it? Surely, I was insane. Right?

CHAPTER 9

LIFE WITHOUT COLOR

All year, Los Angeles is warm and sunny. Driving across the city, it can be difficult to recall what season it is. People are wearing sunglasses and drinking cool drinks through straws everywhere you turn, smiling and laughing beneath the clear blue sky. But in January 2008, even in California, it seemed like winter because I was alone and freezing, and I was hospitalised. I probably shouldn't confess it, but I was a wreck. I was on a high dose of Adderall. I was terrible, and I will acknowledge that I made mistakes. I was furious at what had happened to Kevin. I'd tried everything with him. I'd given everything I had. And he'd turned against me.

I'd begun dating a photographer. I was completely smitten by him. He'd been a paparazzo, and I knew many suspected him of wrongdoing, but all I could see at the time was that he was gallant and helped me out when the others became too pushy. Back then, if I didn't like anything, I would absolutely let you know. And I would do it without hesitation. (If I was hit in the face in Vegas, as I was in July 2023, I would have smacked the individual back 100 percent.) I had no dread. The photographers were continually following us. The chases were absolutely insane—they were both fierce and amusing at times. Many of the photographers were attempting to make me look horrible in order to capture the money shot that said, "Oh, she's lost and she looks crazy right now." But they also wanted me to appear good at times. The photographer and I were being pursued one day, and it was one of those times with him that I'll never forget. We were driving quickly, close to the edge of a cliff, and for some reason, I decided to execute a 360 right there on the edge. I honestly had no idea I could perform a 360—that was utterly beyond me, so I attribute it to God. But I became stuck; the back wheels of the car came to a halt on what appeared to be the very edge, and if the wheels had rotated just three more times, we would have fallen down the cliff.

I looked at him, and he looked back.

"We could have just died," I pointed out.

I was so lively. "Stay safe," we remind our children all the time. Don't do either of these." But, while safety is paramount, I believe it is equally critical to have awakenings and challenge ourselves to feel liberated, to be brave, and to experience what the world has to offer. I had no idea the photographer was married; I had no idea I was effectively his mistress. I only found out after we'd split up. I'd just thought he was a lot of fun, and our time together had been quite heated. He was ten years my senior. The photographers were wherever I went—and I went out a lot for a spell. Despite all of the claims about my being out of control, I don't believe I was ever out of control in a way that justified what happened next. The reality is that I was quite sad and missed my children while they were with Kevin. The photographer assisted me in overcoming my sadness. I yearned for attention, and he provided it to me. It was purely a sexual relationship. My family didn't like him, but I didn't like a lot of things about them. I was encouraged to rebel by the photographer. He still loved me even though he let me sow my oats. He loved me completely. It wasn't like my mother was yelling at me for going out. He went on to say, "Girl, go, you got it, do your thing!" He wasn't like my father, who made enormous demands on his affection. So with the photographer's help, I did my thing completely. And being that daring seemed radical. That was far from what everyone expected of me.

I was speaking as if I were insane. I was obnoxious everywhere I went, including restaurants. People would take me out to lunch, and I would lie down on the table. It was my way of shouting "Fuck you!" to anybody who crossed my path. I mean, I'll own it: I was bad. Or perhaps I wasn't so much evil as angry. I wished to flee. I didn't have any children, and I needed to stay away from the press and photographers. I needed to get out of LA, so the photographer and I took a trip to Mexico. It was as if I'd escaped to a secure haven. Outside my door, there would be a million people everywhere else. But even though I was only gone for a brief period, I felt disconnected from everything. This helped; I felt better for a short time. I should have taken use of it more. My relationship with the photographer appeared to be becoming more serious, and as this occurred, I sensed that my family was trying to draw closer to me—in an unsettling way. "Britney, we feel like something's going on," my mother stated one day. We've heard the cops are after you. "Let's go to the beach."

"The cops are after me?" I said. "For what?" I'd done nothing illegal. That I was certain of. I'd had my ups and downs. I'd had my wild phase. I'd been high on Adderall and had been acting nuts. But I didn't commit any crimes. In fact, as she was aware, I'd spent the previous two days with women. My mother and I had spent the night with my cousin Alli and two other women.

"Just come over to the house!" she exclaimed. "We want to talk to you."

So I accompanied them to their home. There, I met the photographer.

My mother was acting strangely.

"Something's up, right?" remarked the photographer when he arrived.

"Yeah," I replied. "Something's really off." There were helicopters flying around the home all of a sudden.

"Is that for me?" I asked my mother. "Is this a joke?"

It wasn't a prank.

Suddenly, a SWAT team of what appeared to be twenty cops arrived at my residence.

"What the fuck did I do?" I kept yelling. "I didn't do anything!"

I knew I'd been acting strangely, but nothing I'd done justified them treating me like a bank robber. There was nothing that justified uprooting my entire life.

I eventually realised that something had changed from the last time I was taken to the hospital for assessment that month. My father had developed a close bond with Louise "Lou" Taylor, whom he idolised. She was at the forefront of the conservatorship's implementation, which would eventually let them manage and take over my career. Lou, who had recently founded a new company called Tri Star Sports & Entertainment Group, was intimately involved in making decisions prior to the conservatorship. She had few genuine clients at the time. She practically built her company on my name and hard work. Conservatorships, also known as guardianships, are often reserved for those who lack mental capacity and are unable to make decisions for themselves. But I was quite functional. I'd just completed my best album to date. I was producing a lot of money for a lot of people, including my father, who I later discovered took a higher income than he paid me. He paid himself over $6 million, while those connected to him received tens of millions more.

The point is, you can have a conservatorship for two months and then let the person get their life back on track, but that wasn't what my father intended. He desired far more.

My father was able to establish two types of conservatorship: "conservatorship of the person" and "conservatorship of the estate." The conservator of the individual is in charge of the conservatee's daily life, including where they reside, what they eat, whether they can drive a car, and what they do. Even though I asked the court to appoint anyone else—and I mean, anyone off the street would have been better—my father was appointed, the same man who used to make me cry when I was a little girl because he talked to himself.

And I was informed in court that I was insane, and I wasn't even permitted to choose my own lawyer.

The conservator of the estate—in my instance, an estate worth tens of millions of dollars at one point—manages the affairs of the conservatee to keep them from being "subject to undue influence or fraud." My father took on this position in collaboration with a lawyer named Andrew Wallet, who would eventually be paid $426,000 per year to block me from my own money. I'd be obliged to pay my court-appointed lawyer, whom I couldn't replace, upwards of $500,000 every year. My father and Lou's staff Robin Greenhill seemed to dominate my life and watch every move I made. I'm a 5-foot-4-inch pop singer who addresses everyone as "sir" and "ma'am." They acted as if I were a criminal or a predator. There were times when I needed my father and sought out him, but he wasn't there. But when it came time for him to be the conservator, he was there! He's always been obsessed with money. I can't claim my mother was any better. She'd pretended to be innocent throughout her two overnight nights with my girlfriends and myself. She'd known they were going to take me away the whole time. I'm confident it was all premeditated, and that my father, mother, and Lou Taylor were all involved. Tri Star was even considering becoming my co-conservator. Later, I discovered that at the time they placed me in conservatorship, on the heels of his bankruptcy, my father was financially indebted to Lou, owing her at least $40,000, which was a large sum for him at the time. That was later referred to in court as a "conflict of interest" by my new counsel, Mathew Rosengart. I was informed shortly after being taken to the hospital against my will that conservatorship paperwork had been filed.

My mother was writing a memoir at the same time when everything was coming apart for me. She wrote about her lovely daughter chopping off her hair and asking how she did it. She described me as "the happiest little girl in the world."

When I made a bad decision, it was as if my mother didn't care. She would use every blunder to promote her book on television.

She wrote it under my name and discussed her parenting of me, my brother, and sister during a time when all three of us kids were a mess. Jamie Lynn was a pregnant adolescent. Bryan was still trying to find his place in the world and was convinced he was failing our father. And I was in a complete meltdown.

When the book was released, she promoted it on every morning show. When I turned on the TV, B-roll from my videos and my shaved head flashed over the screen. My mother told Meredith Vieira on Today that she'd spent hours worrying what had gone wrong with me. On another show, the audience applauded when she revealed that my sister was pregnant at the age of sixteen. That was evidently elegant as crap, because she was still with the father! Yes, she was married to her spouse and expecting a child at the age of seventeen. They're still married! Great! It makes no difference that she is a child carrying a child!

My mother was telling the audience, "Oh yeah, and here's... Britney," during one of the lowest periods of my life.

And every presentation featured photographs of myself with my head shaved on the screen.

The book meant a lot to her, and it was all at my expense. The timing was out of this world.

I'm willing to acknowledge that in the midst of terrible postpartum depression, my husband's abandonment, the agony of being separated from my two babies, the death of my adored aunt Sandra, and the relentless drumbeat of paparazzi pressure, I'd begun to think like a child.

And yet, when I think back on the worst things I did at the time, I don't think the sum of them is anywhere as cruel as what my mother did by writing and promoting that book.

She was on morning talk shows attempting to hawk her book about how I was driven nuts by being separated from my babies for weeks on end while in hospitals. She was profiting from that gloomy period.

I wasn't the brightest bulb on the tree back then. That is the truth. But many people said after reading my mother's book, "Oh, Britney's so bad." Her book even convinced me that I was awful! And she did that at a moment when I was already feeling so ashamed.

I swear to God, it makes me want to cry just thinking about my children going through anything difficult like I did when they were babies. Do you think I'd write a book about it if one of my sons was going through something similar?

I'd collapse to my knees. I'd do anything to help him get through it, to hug him, to make it better. The last thing I'd do is chop my hair into a bob, put on a nice suit, and sit across from Meredith fucking Vieira on a morning-show set to profit from my child's tragedy. On Instagram, I occasionally spew venom. People don't understand why I'm so angry at my parents. But I believe they would understand if they were in my position.

CHAPTER 10

CONTROL

The conservatorship was reportedly established because I was unable to do anything, including feed myself, spend my own money, or be a mother. So why would they have me film an episode of How I Met Your Mother a few weeks later, followed by a gruelling globe tour? After the conservatorship began, my mother and my brother's girlfriend got short haircuts and went out to dinner drinking wine—paparazzi were there taking pictures of them. Everything felt pre-planned. My father had taken my partner away from me, and I was unable to drive. My mother and father stripped me of my feminine identity. For them, it was a win-win situation. After all my accomplishments and everything I'd done, I was still surprised that the state of California would let a man like my father—an alcoholic, someone who'd declared bankruptcy, failed in business, and terrified me as a child—control me. I thought about the advice my father had given me throughout the years that I had ignored, and I wondered if I would be able to do so again. My father presented the conservatorship as a key step in my "comeback." I'd only recently released the best record of my career, but that was fine. "She's great now!" I heard my father say. She is employed by us! It's an incredible opportunity for our family."

Was it useful to me? Was it perfect for him?

What a great time! I paused. I can return to work as if nothing had happened! Too sick to choose my own guy, yet healthy enough to appear on sitcoms and morning shows and perform for thousands of people around the world every week!

From that point forward, I began to suspect that he saw me as being placed on the planet solely to increase their financial flow. My father turned my modest study and bar area into his office at home. There was a dish with a slew of receipts. Yes, I admit it: I was a nerd who kept all of my receipts in a bowl. To keep track of my tax deductions, I would manually sum up my expenses each week. Even while I was going through a difficult time, the core of who I was as a person remained. That bowl of receipts demonstrated to me that I was still capable of managing my affairs. I've known musicians who smoked drugs, fought, and threw televisions out hotel windows. Not only was I not stealing, causing violence, or using illegal drugs, but I was also keeping track of my tax deductions. That is no longer the case. My father moved his items to the bar and pushed my receipt dish away. "I just wanted to let you know," he said, "that I make all of the decisions.""You sit in that chair, and I'll tell you what's going on."

As I stared at him, I became increasingly afraid.

"I'm Britney Spears now," he said.

On the rare occasions when I went out, such as to my agent and friend Cade's house for a dinner party, the security team would go through the house before I arrived to ensure there was no alcohol, drugs, or even Tylenol. No one at the gathering was permitted to consume alcohol until I left. The other attendees were all great sports about it, but I had a feeling that the actual party began the moment I departed. When someone wanted to date me, my father's security staff would perform a background check on him, make him sign an NDA, and even have him submit to a blood test. (My father also stated I couldn't see the photographer I'd been dating again.) Robin would tell the man about my medical and sexual history before a date. To be clear, this occurred prior to the first date. The experience was humiliating, and I know that the system's lunacy prevented me from finding basic companionship, having a great night out, or making new friends—let alone falling in love. Thinking back on how my father was raised by June and how he raised me, I knew from the start that having him in control would be a nightmare. I was terrified of my father taking control of any area of my life. But taking control of everything? It was the worst thing that could have happened to my music, career, and sanity.

I promptly contacted the strange-as-hell lawyer the court had selected for me and requested for his assistance. Despite the fact that I hadn't selected him, he was all I really had. I was advised that I couldn't hire somebody new since my lawyer had to be approved by the court. Much later, I would discover it was nonsense: I had no idea for thirteen years that I could have hired my own lawyer. I had the impression that the court-appointed lawyer was uninterested in assisting me in understanding what was going on or in fighting for my rights. My mother, who is best friends with Louisiana's governor, could have called him and he would have told me I could hire my own lawyer. But mom kept it a secret; instead, she hired a lawyer for herself so she could continue battling with my father, as she had done when I was younger. I resisted several times, especially when my father took away my cell phone. I'd smuggle in a private phone and try to escape. But they were continuously catching me. And here's the terrible, honest truth: I didn't have much fight left in me after everything I'd been through. I was exhausted and terrified. After being restrained on a gurney, I realised they could restrain my body at any time. They may have tried to kill me, I reasoned. I began to worry if they truly intended to murder me. When my father said, "I call the shots," I thought to myself, "This is too much for me." But I couldn't see an escape. So I felt my spirit withdraw and went into autopilot mode. If I play along, they'll probably see how good I am and let me leave. As a result, I went along with it.

Felicia was still there after I married Kevin and had my children; I had always adored her, but once I stopped touring and started working less, we lost touch. There was talk of Felicia returning for the Circus Tour, but I never had her as my helper again. My father later informed me that I no longer wanted her to work for me. But I never said anything like that. I would never have said no if I had known she wanted to do something for me. My father was hiding her from me without my knowledge. I never saw some of my closest friends again, and I still haven't. It caused me to shut down even more psychologically than before. My parents had some old friends from my hometown come to see me to cheer me up.

"No, thanks," I replied.

I mean, I adored them, but they had children and had moved on with their lives. Their visit to meet me felt more like a gesture of pity than a social invitation. Help is beneficial, but only if it is requested. No way if it doesn't feel like a choice. It's difficult for me to revisit this worst period of my life and consider what may have been different if I'd fought harder back then. That is something I despise even

82

thinking about. To be honest, I can't afford it. I've been through a lot. And it was true that I had been partying when the conservatorship occurred. That was too much for my body to bear. It was time to relax. But I went from being a big partier to a total hermit. I did nothing during the conservatorship. I was with the photographer one day, driving my car quickly and living so much. And then I found myself alone, doing nothing, and not even having access to my own cell phone. It was as if it were night and day. In my previous life, I had the flexibility to make my own decisions, to create my own schedule, to wake up and select how to spend my day. Even the difficult days were difficult for me. After I gave up the struggle, I would wake up every morning and ask myself, "What are we doing?"

And then I'd do as I was told. When I was alone at night, I tried to find inspiration in beautiful or moving music, movies, or books— anything to help numb the agony of this arrangement. I'd hunt for other universes to escape into, just like I did as a child. Every request seemed to go through my father and Robin. They decided where I went and who I went with. Security guards brought me packed envelopes of medication and watched me take them under Robin's supervision. My iPhone now has parental controls. Everything was examined and monitored. Everything. I'd get to bed early. Then I'd wake up and repeat what they'd told me. Once again. Once again. It was like seeing Groundhog Day all over again. That's what I did for thirteen years.

If you're asking why I went along with it, there's one very good reason. I did it for my kids. Because I played by the rules, I was reunited with my boys. It was an ecstatic experience getting to hold them again. When they fell asleep next to me that first night we had back together, I felt whole for the first time in months. I just stared at them sleeping and felt so, so lucky. To see them as much as possible, I did everything I could to appease Kevin. I paid his legal bills, plus child support, plus thousands more a month so the kids could come along with me on the Circus Tour. Within the same short period of time, I appeared on Good Morning America, did the Christmas-tree lighting in Los Angeles, shot a segment for Ellen, and toured through Europe and Australia. But again, the question was nagging at me—if I was so sick that I couldn't make my own decisions, why did they think it was fine for me to be out there smiling and waving and singing and dancing in a million time zones a week?

I'll tell you one good reason. The Circus Tour grossed more than $130 million. Lou Taylor's company, Tri Star, got 5 percent. And I learned, after the conservatorship, that even when I was on hiatus in 2019 and money wasn't coming in, my father paid them an extra minimum "flat fee," so they were paid hundreds of thousands of dollars more. My father got a percentage, too, plus, throughout the conservatorship, about $16,000 a month, more than he'd ever made before. He profited heavily from the conservatorship, becoming a multimillionaire. My freedom in exchange for naps with my children—it was a trade I was willing to make. There is nothing I love more—nothing more important to me on this earth—than my children. I'd lay down my life for them. So, I thought, why not my freedom?

CHAPTER 11

EXCHANGE

How do you hold on to hope? I had resolved to comply with the conservatorship for the sake of my sons, but being a part of it was really difficult. I knew there was something more inside of me, but it was diminishing by the day. The fire within me died out over time. My eyes lost their light. I know my admirers saw it, even if they didn't really comprehend what had occurred because I was so tightly controlled. I feel a lot of sympathy for the woman I was before being placed in the conservatory, while I was recording Blackout. Despite being described as a wayward and wild girl, all of my best work was completed during that period. Overall, however, it was a miserable period. I had two small children, and every time I tried to see them, there was a conflict. Looking back, I believe that if I had been wise, I would have done nothing but focus on my life at home, no matter how difficult it was. At the time, he would say, "Well, if you meet me this weekend, we'll have a two-hour meeting and we'll do this and that and I might let you see the boys a little bit more." Everything felt like a bargain with the devil to acquire what I desired. Yes, I was rebelling, but I can see now that there is a reason why people resist.

And you must allow people to travel through them. I'm not saying I was wrong to spiral, but I don't think it's healthy to hamper someone's spirit to that extent and to tear them down to the point where they no longer feel like themselves. We, as individuals, must put the world to the test. You must push your limits in order to discover who you are and how you want to live. That freedom was granted to others, and by others, I mean men. We believed male rockers were cooler because they arrived late to award presentations. Male pop artists were sleeping with a lot of ladies, which was fantastic. Kevin left me alone with two babies to go use marijuana and make a rap song called "Popozo," which is Portuguese slang for "big ass." Then he took them away from me, and he was named Dad of the Year by Details magazine. A paparazzo who hounded and tortured me for months sued me for $230,000 after I ran over his foot with my car one time while fleeing him. We came to an agreement, and I had to give him a large sum of money. It was considered sweet when Justin cheated on me and then pretended to be sexy. But when I wore a sparkly bodysuit, I had Diane Sawyer on national television making me cry, MTV making me listen to people critiquing my costumes, and a governor's wife screaming she wanted to shoot me.

Growing up, I'd been eyeballed a lot. Since I was a youngster, I'd been scrutinised and had people tell me what they thought of my body. My methods of resistance included shaving my head and acting out. But, as a result of the conservatorship, I was made to believe that those days were over. I needed to grow my hair out and get in shape. I had to get to bed early and take whatever medication they prescribed. If I thought getting ridiculed about my body in the news was awful, hearing it from my own father stung even more. He told me over and over that I looked obese and that I needed to do something about it. So I would put on my sweatpants and head to the gym every day. I'd dabble in some creative endeavours here and there, but my heart wasn't in it anymore. My passion for singing and dancing seemed almost comical at the time. A child's soul is crushed when he or she believes they are never good enough. He'd instilled that message in me as a child, and he was still doing so even after I'd done so much. I wanted to inform my father that you had ruined my life. You're making me work for you now. I'll do it, but damn me if I put my heart into it. I turned into a robot. But not just any robot—a child-robot. I'd become so infantilized that I'd lost track of what made me feel like myself. I would refuse anything my father or mother commanded me to do. My feminine pride would not allow me to take it seriously. The conservatorship took away my womanhood and turned me into a child. Onstage, I became more of an entity than a person. They took away my ability to feel music in my bones and blood. If they had allowed me to live my life, I know I would have followed my heart and gotten out of this the proper way. Thirteen years passed while I felt like a shadow of myself. I feel terrible thinking about my father and his associates having power over my body and my money for so long. Consider how many male artists blew all their money on gambling, and how many struggled with substance abuse or mental illness. Nobody attempted to take away their authority over their bodies or their money. What my family did to me was unjust. The point was, even though I was purportedly unable to care for myself, I accomplished a lot.

I received over twenty honours in 2008, including the Cosmopolitan Ultimate Woman of the Year Award. I won three Moonmen at the VMAs, just one year after being criticised for my "Gimme More" performance. "Piece of Me" won every category in which it was nominated, including Video of the Year. I thanked God, my sons and my followers for their support. I found it almost amusing that I got those accolades for the record I made while apparently being so incapacitated that I had to be controlled by my family. But, when I paused to think about it for a long time, it wasn't hilarious at all. While I was generally unhappy, I was able to find joy and comfort in my boys and my routine on a daily basis. I made new buddies. Jason Trawick was a guy I dated. He was ten years older than me and seemed to have his life in order. I liked that he wasn't a performer but an agent, so he understood the business and my life. We were together for three years. He was hypervigilant when we went out together. I was aware that I may be clueless at times. (I'm no longer clueless. I'm basically a CIA agent now.) He was constantly scrutinising everything and excessively regulating situations. I'd spent so much time around the paparazzi that I knew what was going on; I knew the arrangement. So seeing him in a suit, working at this massive agency, and getting in the car with me made me feel like he was almost too conscious of who I was. He was very concerned with management. I was used to cameras swarming me on the streets, and I scarcely noticed them any longer, which isn't always a bad thing. We had a fantastic friendship. I felt a great deal of love for and from him. I was still psychologically damaged as a result of everything that had transpired with Kevin and my children, as well as living under the constraints of the conservatorship my father had established. I lived in Thousand Oaks, California. My children were small at the time, and my father still had control over my life. Even though I was on a sabbatical following the Femme Fatale Tour, my father questioned everything I did, including what I ate. It perplexed me that my mother never mentioned it—my parents reconciled in 2010, eight years after their divorce. And the state of California had betrayed me. My mother seemed to like the fact that, thanks to the conservatorship, my father now had a legitimate job. Every single night, they sat on the couch and watched Criminal Minds. Who would do that?

When my father told me I couldn't have dessert, I felt like it was not just him but my entire family and state informing me, as if I wasn't legally permitted to eat dessert because he said no. I eventually began to wonder, "Wait, where am I?" Nothing made sense any longer. I returned to work because I felt I needed more direction. I attempted to keep myself busy by being industrious. I started appearing on more TV series, including The X Factor in 2012. Many people, such as Christina Aguilera and Gwen Stefani, I believe, are really professional on television. They thrive when the camera is on them. That's fantastic. I used to be able to do that when I was younger, but when I'm terrified, I feel like I'm ageing backwards. So I got to the point where I was quite nervous if I knew I had to go on air, and I didn't like being nervous all day. Perhaps I'm no longer cut out for it. That's okay with me now that I've accepted it. People that try to push me in that direction will get a firm no from me. I've been humiliated and pushed to do things I didn't want to do. It's not my thing right now. That's one thing if you got me a nice cameo on a fun TV show where I'm in and out in a day, but acting doubtful for eight hours straight while evaluating people on TV? No, thank you. It irritated me to no end. It was at this time when I proposed to Jason. He helped me get through a lot of difficult times. But, not long after he became my co-conservator in 2012, my feelings shifted. I couldn't see it at the time, but having him involved with the institution that controls my life may have played a role in taking the romanticism out of our relationship. I recognized that I didn't have any negative thoughts toward him, but I also didn't love him anymore. I no longer slept in the same room as him. I just wanted to cuddle with my children. I felt such a connection with them. I literally shut the door on him.

"That is abhorrent," my mother responded.

"I'm sorry, I can't help it," I explained. "I don't love him anymore like that."

He broke up with me, but I didn't care because I'd grown tired of him. He wrote me a lengthy letter and then vanished. When our relationship ended, he resigned as my co-conservator. He appeared to be going through an identity crisis to me. He dyed his hair, went to the Santa Monica Pier, and rode bikes with a group of tattooed males every day. Hey, I understand. I'm having my own identity issue now that I'm in my forties. I believe it was simply time for us to part ways.

We were not permitted to drink during the conservatorship excursions because they were totally sober. I formerly had most of the same dancers as Christina Aguilera. Christina and the dancers and I met in Los Angeles. She appeared to be in a lot of trouble. But the dancers and I ended up swimming in a lovely pool and relaxing in a Jacuzzi. It would have been fantastic to drink with them and be rebellious, sarcastic, and fun. I couldn't do it because my life had devolved into a Sunday-school Bible church camp under the conservatorship. They transformed me into a teenager in some ways, and a female in others. But sometimes I felt like an imprisoned adult lady who was always irritated. This is what's difficult to explain: how quickly I could vary between being a small girl, a teenager, and a woman as a result of how they had deprived me of my independence. There was no way for me to act like an adult because they wouldn't treat me like an adult, so I would regress and act like a little girl, but then my adult self would step back in—but my world wouldn't let me be an adult. For a long time, the woman in me was suppressed. They wanted me to be wild onstage, as they instructed, and a robot the rest of the time. I felt robbed of life's good secrets—those essential claimed faults of gluttony and experience that make us human. They sought to remove the uniqueness and make things as routine as possible. It was the end of my artistic talent.

Back in the studio, I wrote one solid song with will.i.am called "Work Bitch." But I wasn't producing much music that I was proud of, possibly because I wasn't interested in it. I was completely discouraged. My father always seemed to choose the darkest and ugliest facilities to record in. Some people seemed to get a kick out of the fact that I didn't notice those things. In those situations, I felt hemmed in; I felt they set me up. They seemed to thrive on my dread, turning it all into drama, which made me sad, and therefore they always won. All I knew was that I needed to work, and I wanted to do the right thing by creating an album that I was proud of. But it was as if I had forgotten how powerful I was. My manager approached me after The X Factor to perform as part of a Las Vegas residency. Why not, I reasoned. My heart was no longer in music recording. I wasn't as intensely driven as I used to be. I couldn't bring any more flames. I was sick of it. I had two children. I'd suffered a nervous breakdown. My parents had taken over my profession. What else could I do at this point but go home?

As a result, I agreed. I went to Vegas like everyone else, hoping to win. Las Vegas's dry heat appealed to me. I liked how everyone trusted in good fortune and the dream. Even when Paris Hilton and I were kicking off our shoes and racing through casinos, I had always appreciated going there. But it seems like a lifetime ago. My residency began just after Christmas in 2013. The boys were seven and eight years old. It was a fantastic gig at first. At first, being onstage in Vegas was amazing. And no one ever let me forget that my residency was a watershed moment for the Strip. I was told that my act brought young people back to Sin City and transformed the scene of Las Vegas entertainment for a new generation. I got so much energy from the fans. I got really good at doing the show. I gained so much confidence, and everything was OK for a while—as wonderful as it could be while I was so tightly controlled. I began dating Charlie Ebersol, a TV producer. He appeared to be marriage material to me: he took excellent care of himself. His family was close to him. I adored him.

Charlie exercised every day, taking pre-workout pills and a slew of vitamins. He told me about his dietary research and began giving me energy pills. That irritated my father. He knew everything I ate and even when I went to the bathroom. So when I began using energy supplements, he saw that I had more energy onstage and was in better form than before. Charlie's programs appeared to be a good thing for me. But I believe my father began to suspect that I had a problem with those energy pills, despite the fact that they were over-the-counter rather than prescription. So he told me I had to stop using drugs and sent me to rehab. He got to decide where and when I went. And going to treatment meant missing out on seeing my kids for a month. The only solace I had was knowing it was only for a month and that I'd be done. He chose Malibu as the location for me. We had to do boxing and other activities outside for hours every day that month because there was no gym. Many of the people at the facility were severely addicted to drugs. I was terrified of being there by myself. At the very least, I was permitted to have a security guard with whom I would have lunch every day.

It was tough for me to comprehend that my father was marketing himself as this amazing guy and devoted grandfather while throwing me away, putting me in a facility with crack and heroin users against my choice. I'll just say it: he was awful. When I came out, I went back to playing acts in Vegas as if nothing had occurred. Part of it was because my father told me I needed to get back out there, and part of it was because I was still so sweet, eager to please, and trying to do the right thing and be a good girl. My father was always observing everything I did. I couldn't operate a vehicle. Everyone that came to my trailer was required to sign waivers. Everything was extremely secure—so secure that I couldn't breathe.

And no matter how hard I tried to lose weight or exercise, my father would always tell me I was obese. He restricted my diet. The irony was that we had a butler, which was a luxury, and I would ask him for genuine meals. "Sir," I'd like to ask, "can you please sneak a hamburger or ice cream to me?"

"Ma'am, I'm sorry," he'd say. "I have strict orders from your father."

So I ate nearly nothing except chicken and canned vegetables for two years. Two years is a long time to go without eating what you want, especially when it's your body, your labour, and your soul that generates the money that everyone relies on. Two years of being told no when I asked for french fries. It was really demeaning to me. It's bad enough that you've put yourself on a rigid diet. But it's made worse when someone denies you the meal you crave. My body no longer felt like mine. I'd go to the gym and feel so out of my mind with this trainer telling me what to do with my body that I felt chilly on the inside. I was terrified. To be honest, I was utterly miserable. It also didn't work. The diet had the opposite impact that my father had hoped for. I put on weight. Even if I wasn't eating as much, he made me feel ugly and inadequate. Perhaps this is due to the power of your thoughts: whatever you believe you are, you become. I was so exhausted by it all that I just gave up. My mother appeared to support my father's plan for me. It always amazed me that so many people felt so at ease discussing my physique. It began when I was young. People, whether strangers in the media or members of my own family, seemed to regard my body as public property: something they could regulate, control, condemn, or use as a weapon. My physique was strong enough to carry two children while yet being agile enough to do every rehearsed action flawlessly onstage. And now here I was, having every calorie tracked so that people might continue to profit from my body.

CHAPTER 12

VEGAS

I enjoyed teaching dancing to youngsters at a studio once a month, which provided me with consolation and optimism during my time in Vegas. I instructed a class of forty children. Then, back in LA, I taught once every two months, not far from my house. That was one of the most enjoyable experiences of my life. It was refreshing to be in a room with youngsters who were free of judgement. Everyone in the conservatory was continually judging anything I did. The excitement and trust of children my age—between five and twelve—is contagious. Their enthusiasm is wonderful. They are eager to learn. Being with children is completely healing for me. I took a turn one day and accidentally hit a tiny little girl in the head with my hand.

"Baby! I'm very sorry!" I said.

I was so upset that I got down on my knees in front of her. I took a band off my finger, one of my favourite rings, and handed it to her, pleading for her forgiveness.

"Miss Britney, it's fine!" she exclaimed. "You didn't even hurt me."

I wanted to do everything I could to show her that I cared if she was in pain and that I would go to any length to make it up to her. Wait a minute, I thought, looking up at her from my knees on the dance studio floor. Why are the people entrusted with my care by the state not half as concerned about my well-being as I am about this little girl's?

I made the decision to fight my way out of the conservatorship. In 2014, I went to court and requested that my father be drug-tested due to his drunkenness and erratic conduct. After all, he was in charge of both my money and my life. But my case was never heard. The judge simply did not pay attention. What followed was a shady attempt to get my own counsel. I even referenced the conservatorship on a chat show in 2016, but that segment of the conversation never aired. Huh. How intriguing. That sense of being trapped aided in the demise of my romantic life. Charlie and I became so arrogant after a dumb dispute that we stopped speaking to each other. It was the stupidest thing I'd ever done. I couldn't force myself to speak to him, and he was too proud to speak to me. That's when I met Julia Michaels and Justin Tranter, two fantastic songwriters. We'd sit together and write everything. I was very enthusiastic about it. It was the one thing I really put my heart into during the conservatorship's thirteen years. I put forth a lot of effort on the tunes, which gave me confidence. You know how you can tell when you're good at something? You start doing something and think to yourself, "I've got this." Writing that record restored my confidence. I finished it and played it for my sons.

"What should I name the album?" I inquired. My children are quite musically savvy.

"Just name it Glory," Sean Preston suggested.

That is exactly what I did. It meant a lot to me to see the kids so happy with their album—I thought, I'm proud of this, too! It was a sensation I hadn't felt in a long time. I launched the video for "Make Me," and I performed at the 2016 VMAs for the first time since 2007. When I first saw Hesam Asghari on the set of my music video for "Slumber Party," I knew he had to be in my life. I was instantly smitten. Initially, we had an unbelievable chemistry. We couldn't keep our hands apart. He addressed me as his lioness. The newspapers were quick to declare that he was cheating on me. We'd only been together for two weeks! We stayed together. My light began to rekindle.My father then felt I needed to go back to therapy since I had snuck my over-the-counter energy pills. He knew I had a problem, but he was gracious enough to admit me as an outpatient as long as I attended Alcoholics Anonymous four times a week. I was hesitant at first, but the women I met there soon inspired me. I thought to myself as I listened to them tell their stories, "These women are brilliant." Their stories were truly heartbreaking. I discovered a human connection in those meetings that I had never known before in my life. So, at first, I enjoyed it a lot. Some of the girls, however, did not always appear. They might choose which meetings to attend. I had no option in the matter. Friends I met there may go once a week or twice a week, or they could go to a morning meeting one day and an evening meeting the next. I was not permitted to make any changes. I had the same meetings at the same time every week, no matter what. I returned home after a long day of shows to discover my sons, my assistant, my mother, and my father.

"Time for your meeting," my father said.

"Is there any way I can just stay at home and watch a movie with the boys right now?" "I've never missed a meeting," I said.

In Vegas, I had never seen a movie with my children. I reasoned that we could prepare popcorn and have a fun time together.

"No, you have to go," he said emphatically.

I turned to face my mother, expecting her to defend me, but she turned aside. At that time, I felt like I was in a cult, with my father as the cult leader. They were treating me as if I were his slave. But, I thought, recalling how hard I worked on those shows, I was so good. I wasn't simply good; I was outstanding. It was a remark that came to mind again and again over the next few years as I reflected on how I had not only met but beyond the expectations that had been set on me—and how unfair it was that I was still not free. I'd worked so hard and followed the schedule they'd set for me—four weeks on, four weeks off. When I was on, I used to do three two-hour shows per week. And, on or off, I followed the weekly plan they devised for me, which included four AA meetings, two hours of treatment, and three hours of training every week, in addition to fan meet-and-greets and three gigs. I was completely fatigued. And I wished to be in control of my own destiny.

"Oh, honey, what are you doing?" one of my hairdressers questioned when she saw my itinerary. Her two girls looked up to her as a mother figure. I liked her a lot.

"You think it's too much?" I asked.

"It's more than too much," she said. "That's insane."

94

She leaned in, as if she needed to tell me something essential. "Listen," she said, directing her audience. "In order to be creative, you must make time in your schedule for play." Having that alone time helps to ground you. You can just stare at the wall if you like. People need it."

Someone else was doing my hair the next day, so whatever she said must have gotten back to my father. That hairstylist was never seen again by me. We girls have hair as performers. That's what real men want to see. They enjoy watching the long hair move. They want you to destroy it. They can tell you're having a good time if your hair is moving. I donned tight wigs and danced in such a way that not a single hair on my head moved throughout the most depressing moments of my Las Vegas residency. Everyone who was earning money off of me wanted me to move my hair, and I was well aware of this—so I did everything but that. When I look back, I realise how much of myself I withheld onstage, how much I punished everyone else by trying to hurt the individuals who held me captive—including my devoted followers and myself. But now I understand why I'd been sleepwalking for the previous thirteen years. I had been traumatised. By holding back onstage, I was attempting to rebel in some manner, even if I was the only one who realised what was going on. As a result, I didn't toss my hair or flirt. I did the dances and sung the notes, but I wasn't as fired up as I had been in the past. My own kind of a factory slowdown was lowering my enthusiasm onstage.

As an artist, I was unable to achieve the sensation of freedom that I had previously experienced. And as artists, we have that freedom in who we are and what we do. Under the conservatorship, I was not free. I aspired to be a world-class woman. I couldn't be a woman while under guardianship. Glory, on the other hand, was a different story. I became more enthusiastic about my performances when the Glory singles became available. I resumed wearing high heels. It came over most powerfully when I wasn't trying so hard and just allowed myself to transcend as a star onstage. And that's when I felt the audience really lift me up.

I began to feel better about myself after promoting Glory. That third year in Vegas, I regained some of my fire. I began to appreciate the glitz of playing every night in Sin City, as well as the spontaneity of feeling alive in front of an audience. Even if I wasn't giving it my all onstage, there were parts of me that began to awaken. I was able to rekindle the bond between a performer and an audience. I have a hard time describing to folks who haven't been onstage what it's like to feel that current between your physical body and the bodies of other people in a room. Electricity is the only metaphor that truly works. You have an electrifying sensation. The energy flows out of you, through the crowd, and back into you in a loop. I'd had to be on autopilot for so long: the only current I could tap was whatever was inside of me that kept me moving. I gradually regained faith in my talents. I didn't tell anyone for a while. I kept it hidden. Just as I'd retreated into my fantasies as a child to escape the craziness of my parents, in Las Vegas, as an adult but with less freedom than I'd had as a child, I began to escape into a new dream—freedom from my family and a return to becoming the artist I knew I possessed. Everything began to appear feasible. Hesam and I were so close that we discussed having a child together. But, being in my thirties, I knew time was running out.

I was swamped with health appointments at the start of the conservatorship. Doctor after doctor—probably twelve doctors a week—visiting my home. Nonetheless, when I requested an appointment to have my IUD removed, my father refused to allow me to go. When the conservatorship was imposed, everything became monitored, with security guards stationed throughout. My entire existence shifted in ways that were maybe safer for me physiologically but were totally disastrous for my feeling of joy and creativity. "Oh, your life was saved!" several others exclaimed. But, no, not at all. It's all about how you look at it. It's all about perception. My music was my life, and the conservatory was lethal because it shattered my soul. Prior to the conservatory, I had been in and out of recording studios. During my conservatory, a team of people kept track of when I went to the bathroom in the recording studio. I'm not exaggerating. After the conservatorship, I discovered that my father and Robin at Lou Taylor's company, Tri Star, had been involved with the security company they hired, Black Box, in monitoring and reviewing calls and texts coming out of and going to my cell phone, including private texts with my boyfriend, my lawyer at the time, and my own children, and that my father had a bug installed in my home. At my own house! Everything was under their control. I left home as a teenager because my family situation was so bad. All those times when I was a little girl and had to go out into the living room and say, "Shut up, Mama!" as my father lay passed out drunk in his chair—those times would come back to me when I woke up and stared at the ceiling, wondering how those people had come to be in charge again. I vowed to do everything I could to get away in those calm periods in the middle of the night.

That third year in Vegas, I felt something inside of me that I hadn't felt in a long, long time. I felt powerful. I realised I had to take action. My body, heart, physique, and spiritual self could no longer accept the conservatorship once I began to return to myself. My small heart finally said, "I'm not going to stand for this."

My parents had convinced me for so long that I was the terrible guy, the insane one, and it had worked well in their advantage. It was a blow to my spirit. They put out my fire. For a decade, I devalued myself. But on the inside, I was yelling at them. You have to comprehend both the helplessness and the anger in that. It irritated me to see my family drinking and having a good time after my gigs when I wasn't even allowed a taste of Jack and Coke. I knew I looked like a star onstage—I was wearing gorgeous tights and high heels—but why the fuck couldn't I sin in Sin City?

As I grew stronger and entered a new period of my womanhood, I began to look for models of how to use power for good. Reese Witherspoon was an excellent role model for me. She's sweet, pleasant, and quite intelligent .When you start to see yourself in that light—not just as someone who lives to make everyone else happy, but as someone who deserves to have their wishes granted—everything changes. When I began to believe that I, like Reese, could be both nice and strong, it altered my perception of who I was. If no one is used to you being forceful, they will be shocked when you start speaking out. I felt myself transforming into their worst nightmare. I was a queen now, and I was beginning to speak up. I envisioned them submitting to me. My power surged back to me. I knew how to present myself. Putting up with that kind of schedule has made me tough. I had no choice but to be powerful, and I believe the audience sensed it. When you demand respect, it says a lot. It alters everything. So when I heard my conservators try to convince me yet again that I was stupid if I sought to decline a performance or find a way to give myself extra time off, I revolted. I told myself, "If you're trying to make me feel bad for saying no, I'm not going to fall for it again."

The residency was scheduled to conclude on December 31, 2017. I couldn't wait any longer. For starters, I had become tired of doing the same show week after week for years. I kept pleading for a remix or a new song to break up the boredom. I'd begun to lose the excitement I'd felt when performing when I was younger. I no longer had the pure, unadulterated passion of singing that I had as a teen. Other people were now telling me what to sing and when to sing it. Nobody appeared to care what I wanted. The message I was getting was that their thoughts were important, but mine should be ignored. I was only there to entertain them and make them money. It was such a waste of time. And, as a performer who has always taken great pride in her skills, I can't express how upset I was that they wouldn't ever allow me to change up my show. In Vegas, we had weeks between each set of concerts. So much time was squandered. I wanted to give my audience something new and exciting by remixing my tunes. They wouldn't let me play my favourite songs, such as "Change Your Mind" or "Get Naked." They seemed to want to shame me rather than allow me to give my audience the best performance possible every night, which they deserved. Instead, I had to perform the same performance every week: the same routines, songs, and arrangements. I'd been performing shows like this for a long time. I was desperate to shake things up, to give my lovely, devoted audience something new and exciting. But all I could hear was "no."

It was strange how sluggish it was. I was concerned about what my admirers thought of me. I could only express how much more I wanted to give them. I used to spend hours in studios doing my own remixes with an engineer. "We can't put remixes in because of the show's time code," they explained. We'd have to start from scratch."

"Redo it!" I exclaimed. I'm known for bringing new ideas to the table, yet they were always dismissive. When I pushed, they stated the best they could do was play one of my new songs in the background while I changed. They pretended to be doing me a tremendous favour by playing my favourite new music while I was underground furiously changing costumes. It was awkward because I am familiar with the industry. I understood it was entirely possible that we could modify the show. It wasn't a priority for my father, who was in control. That meant that the people who would be required to make it happen would simply refuse to do so. My body felt elderly after singing such outdated renditions of songs. I was craving new sounds and action. I now believe that the fact that I was the star intimidated them. My father, on the other hand, was in charge of the star. Me.

I felt so light and free when I was filming the visuals for Glory's singles. Glory brought up memories of how it felt to perform new stuff and how much I needed it. When I found out I'd be receiving the first-ever Radio Disney Icon Award the year after Glory was released, I thought to myself, This is fantastic! I'll take the boys and wear a gorgeous black dress, and we'll have a great time. As I sat in the crowd, watching a mashup of my songs played, I was overcome with emotion. I was a ball of emotion by the time Jamie Lynn made a surprise appearance to sing "Till the World Ends" and gave me my prize.

I kept flashing back to the concert special I'd done for In the Zone while watching the show. It was an ABC program that had been remixed. I'd been practising for a week and had sung numerous new songs. They took really great pictures of me. I was like a kid. To be honest, it's some of my best work. A sensual performance of "... Baby One More Time" had a Cabaret feel to it, and for "Everytime," I wore a lovely white outfit. It was really breathtakingly lovely. It felt amazing to be at that point in my career, free and presenting my music in my own unique style, with complete creative control.

And, even though I was honoured by the performances, I was enraged as I accepted the Icon Award at the Radio Disney Music Awards. Three vocalists and my sister were making new arrangements—something I had pleaded for for thirteen years—having fun with my songs in ways I hadn't seen in hundreds of performances, and I couldn't help but smile. Cade, my friend and agent, used to contact me and say we should go on a road trip, and I'd be in the car before he finished telling me where we were going. If I wanted the volume turned up at one of my gigs, I'd gently request that the sound guy do so. If you irritated me, everyone would know about it. I felt like a badass. But in Vegas, I merely smiled and nodded and repeated the same show like a windup doll. The fact that I'd have two vacations with my kids, like I did every year, was the only thing keeping me going. But the year Glory was released, I had to tour instead, which meant I couldn't go on vacation; I had to bring the kids on tour with me, which wasn't fun for anyone. So I really needed those holidays the next year. My team came in one night before a show and I flagged it for them: "Hey," I said, "I just wanted to give you a heads-up." This year, I really need those getaways."

Tradition is extremely important to me. My and my children's favourite activity was to travel to Maui, rent a boat, and sail out into the ocean. To be honest, it's for my mental health.

"If there's a large amount of money," the members of my group stated, "we'll go and do, like, two tour shows, and then you can come back and have the whole summer off."

"Great!" I exclaimed. "We're on the same page."

A few months passed. In December 2017, Vegas was finally coming to an end. I was overjoyed. I've performed in hundreds of performances. While I was changing between performances in my dressing area, someone from my crew approached me and said, "Hey, yeah, so you're going on tour this year after Vegas ends." We can't just leave it at Vegas. We need to finish it on tour this summer."

"That wasn't part of the deal," I explained. "I told you, I'm taking the kids to Maui."

When I tried to compromise, the conversation quickly became heated. Finally, one of my team members stated, "If you don't go on tour, you will end up in court, because you have a contract." They were threatening me, I realised. And they were aware of how upsetting it was for me to be in court. I eventually calmed down. I began to think that if it was only a few weeks, it wouldn't be so horrible. Then I could return and still enjoy some of the summer. We might simply go to Maui later. This proved to be far too hopeful. The tour was a living nightmare. I'm sure the dancers felt it as well. My father's terms had us more bound than ever before. We had to give the security crew two hours' notice just to exit the room. To make matters worse, I was still artistically inhibited, doing the same old thing. They were still not allowing me to rework my songs or change up the show. We could have adjusted the show and created something good, something new that would have felt new to the audience, as well as to me and the dancers. That was the one concession I requested, and they said no as usual. Because if I genuinely took charge of my show, people might realise that I don't need my father as a conservator. He seemed to enjoy making me feel "less than." It gave him authority. I cried when I saw my pets when I arrived home since I'd missed them so much. I began to arrange a trip with the boys to make up for the time we'd lost. I explained to my team, "We'll give you three weeks off and then we have to start rehearsing for a new Vegas show."

"Three weeks?" I inquired. "I was supposed to have all summer!"

I'd detested the tou r.It was as if I had been told that the weekend would never come. I could already hear the screaming. Outside, hundreds of people had gathered. A large throng gathered outside the new Park MGM hotel in Las Vegas on an October day in 2018. Superfans wore similar outfits and waved flags with the word B on them. Onstage, dancers were wearing BRITNEY T-shirts. Announcers were live streaming their excitement to their followers. The laser lights flashed. A massive screen displayed scenes from my videos. Dance music was blasting. A parade passed past, with marchers screaming songs like "My loneliness is killing me!"

The lights were turned off.

"We are here to welcome the new queen of Vegas," Mario Lopez, who was on hand to host the event, shouted over the microphone. The dramatic music began with a riff from "Toxic." Crazy lights flashed on the Park MGM, giving the impression that the structure was pulsing. Cue a medley of other tunes and images of a rocket ship, a helicopter, a circus large top, and a snake in Eden. Fire erupted from fire pits all around the stage! "... I climbed from the floor on a hydraulic lift, waving and smiling in a tight little black dress with star cutouts and tassels, my hair extra long and blond. Mario Lopez continued, "Ladies and gentlemen, Britney Spears!"

In my high heels, I strolled down the stairs to "Work Bitch" and signed a few autographs for admirers. But then I did something surprising. I strolled right by the cameras. I continued walking till I got into an SUV and drove away. I remained silent. I did not deliver. You were undoubtedly wondering what just happened if you were watching. What you didn't witness was my father and his staff attempting to bully me into announcing the show. I'd stated I didn't want to announce it because I didn't want to do it, as I'd been saying for months. I had no concept of what overprotection was when I sang "Overprotected" so many years ago. I'd find out soon enough, because once I made it plain that I wasn't going to do Vegas anymore, my family had me leave. I was feeling very good as the holidays neared. Aside from my concern that my father was planning something, the women I'd met at AA made me feel strong and encouraged. They were bright, but they also had a lot of common sense, and I'd learned a lot from them about how to be an adult woman who navigated the world with honesty and boldness. Hesam took me somewhere special for my birthday. I began making holiday plans, but my father insisted on taking the boys for Christmas. I'd have to see my father as well if I wanted to see them. "The boys don't want to be with you this year," my father stated when I resisted. They're returning to Louisiana with me and your mother, and that's the end of it."

"This is news to me," he replied, "but if they'd really rather be in Louisiana that week, I guess that's okay."

The Vegas event had not yet been cancelled. I was hiring new dancers and reviewing routines. I'd been working with all the dancers—new and old—at a rehearsal one day when one of the dancers who'd been with the show for four years did a move for us all. When I saw it, I winced; it looked quite difficult. "I don't want to do that one," that's what I said. "It's too hard."

It didn't seem like much of a concern to me until my team and the directors abruptly disappeared into a room and locked the door. I had the impression that I had done something terrible, but I couldn't see how not wanting to complete one move in a routine could count as such. I mean, I was about five years older than when the previous residency began, and my physique had altered as well. What difference did it make if we switched things up?

From what I could gather, we'd all been having a good time. I suffer from social anxiety, therefore anything that makes me feel uneasy comes to me first. But everything seemed fine that day. I was laughing and conversing with the dancers. Some of the newcomers could do gainers, which is a standing back tuck in the future. They were fantastic! When I inquired whether I could learn it, one of them offered to tutor me. That is to say, we were both playing and conversing. Nothing seemed to be going wrong. But the way my crew had acted had me concerned that something was wrong. My doctor addressed me the next day in therapy.

"We found energy supplements in your purse," that's what he stated. The energy vitamins offered me a boost of confidence and vigour, and they didn't require a prescription. He was aware that I had been using them throughout my Vegas gigs, but he made a huge deal out of it now.

"We feel like you're doing way worse things behind our backs," he went on to say. "We also don't think you're doing well in rehearsals." You're making life difficult for everyone."

"Is this a joke?" I inquired.

I was immediately enraged. I've worked so hard. My work ethic was excellent.

"We're going to admit you to a facility," the therapist explained. "And before you go to this place, over Christmas break, we're going to have a woman come to run psychological tests on you."

A showy doctor, whom I had seen on TV and despised, came to my house against my will, sat me down, and assessed my cognitive ability for hours. My father informed me that this doctor had determined that I had failed the tests: "She stated you failed. You must now visit a mental health centre. Something is seriously wrong with you. But don't worry, we've located a tiny recovery facility in Beverly Hills for you. It will only set you back $60,000 every month."

As I gathered my belongings, crying, I wondered how long I should pack and how long they'd make me remain. But I was assured that there was no way to find out. "Perhaps a month." Perhaps two months. Perhaps three months. It all depends on how effectively you perform and demonstrate your ability." The program was allegedly a "luxury" rehab that had designed a customised curriculum for me, so I wouldn't have to deal with other people.

"What if I don't go?" I inquired.

My father warned me that if I didn't go, I'd have to go to court and be humiliated. "We will make you look like a fucking idiot, and trust me, you will not win," he warned. It's better if I tell you to go than if a judge tells you."

It felt like blackmail and I was being gaslighted. They seemed to be attempting to kill me. In all those years, I had never stood up to my father; I had never said no to anyone. My no in that room that day truly irritated my father. They made me go. I had no choice because they had my back to the wall. If you don't do it, this is what will happen to you, so we recommend you do it now. But that didn't happen—getting it over with. Because I couldn't leave once I was there, no matter how much I begged. They had me imprisoned against my will for months.

CHAPTER 13

I WANT TO BE FREE

The physicians whisked me away from my children, dogs, and home. I was unable to go outside. I couldn't operate a vehicle. I had to give blood once a week. I couldn't take a bath alone. I was unable to close the door to my room. Even as I was changing, I was being watched. At nine p.m., I had to go to bed. They watched TV with me in bed from eight to nine o'clock. Every morning at eight o'clock, I had to get up. Every day was filled with meetings. I sat in a chair for several hours a day, receiving obligatory therapy. I passed the time between appointments by peering out the window, watching automobiles pull up and drive away, so many cars delivering so many therapists, security guards, physicians, and nurses. What I think hurt me the most was watching all those people come and go while I was unable to go. Everything that was occurring to me was for my own good, I was informed. But I felt abandoned in that environment, and even though everyone said they were there to help me, I never understood what my family expected from me. I completed all of my responsibilities. On weekends, my kids would come over for an hour. But I wouldn't be able to visit them if I didn't do what I was "supposed to do" throughout the week. Cade was one of the few people that phoned me. Cade has always made me feel protected while also putting me in danger. The most amusing call I received the entire time was him FaceTiming me from a hospital in Texas to tell me about being bitten by a scorpion in his bed—in his bed. His leg ballooned to the size of a basketball.

"Are you serious right now?" Looking at his swollen leg on my phone, I murmured. It was shockingly bad. Cade's bad leg provided one of the few genuine distractions from what I was going through, and I'll be eternally thankful to him and that Texas scorpion.

The therapists interrogated me for hours on end, every day, seven days a week. I'd been on Prozac for years, but in the hospital, they quickly yanked me off it and put me on lithium, a dangerous drug that makes you exceedingly slow and sleepy and that I didn't want or need. My sense of time began to shift, and I became bewildered.

When I was on lithium, I had no idea where I was or even who I was. My mind wasn't working as it used to. It wasn't lost on me that my grandmother Jean, who eventually committed suicide, had been put on lithium in Mandeville.

Meanwhile, my long-term security crew treated me as if I were a criminal. When it came time for blood draws, the tech would be surrounded by the nurse, a security guard, and my assistant. Is it true that I was a cannibal? Is it true that I was a bank robber? Was I a savage beast? Why was I treated as if I was about to burn down the place and murder everyone?

They took my blood pressure three times a day, as if I were an eighty-year-old lady. They'd also take their time. Please make me sit. Obtain the cuff. Attach it gradually. Slowly increase the pressure... Every day, three times. I needed to move around to feel normal. As a dancer, movement was my existence. It fed my soul. I sought it and needed it. But they held me in that chair for what seemed like an eternity. I started to feel like I was being tortured ritually. I was nervous in my feet, my heart, and my mind. I'd never be able to expend that much energy. You know how when your body moves, it reminds you that you're alive? That was all I desired. And because I couldn't move, I began to worry whether I was already half-dead. I was devastated. My ass grew so large from sitting in a chair for hours on end that none of my shorts fit anymore. I grew disconnected from my own body. I had horrible nightmares about running through a forest, dreams that were so real. Please wake up, please wake up, please wake up—I don't want it to be real, I'm sure this is only a dream. If my intention in going there was to heal, that was not the result. I started picturing myself as a bird without wings. You know how, as a youngster, you'd run around with your arms spread and, with the wind rushing over your arms, you'd feel like you were flying for a split second? That was the sensation I desired. Instead, I felt like I was sinking into the soil every day.

In Beverly Hills, I completed the program on my own for two months. It was horrible, like I was in my own horror film. I enjoy watching scary movies. I saw The Conjuring. After six months at the treatment clinic, I'm not afraid of anything. I'm not afraid of anything now. I'm probably the least afraid woman alive right now, but that doesn't make me strong; it makes me sad. I shouldn't be this powerful. Those months hardened me. I miss being what we used to call a sass ass in Kentwood. My sassiness was lost throughout my stay in the hospital. It shattered my spirit in so many ways. The most difficult thing was believing that I had to act fine in front of the physicians and visitors at all times. If I became agitated, it was interpreted as proof that I wasn't progressing. I was out of control and insane if I became upset and expressed myself. It reminded me of how they used to test people to see whether they were witches in the earlier days. They were going to dump the woman into a pond. She was a witch and would be slain if she floated. If she drowned, she was innocent, so whatever. She was already dead, but I suppose they believed it was still worth knowing what kind of lady she'd been.

After a few months, I called my father and begged him to let me return home.

"I'm sorry," he replied, "the judge will have to figure out what she's going to do with you." Right now, it's up to the doctors. I'm afraid I'm powerless to assist you. I'm referring you to the physicians because I can't help you."

My father had sent me a pearl necklace and a beautiful handwritten message for Christmas before they put me in that situation. Why is he doing this, I wondered? What is his name?

What stung me the most was that he'd been stating in front of the cameras for years, whether it was when I did the "Work Bitch" video or when the conservatorship first began and we did the Circus Tour, that he was all about me and the guys.

"That's my baby girl!" he exclaimed into the camera. "I love her so much." I was confined in a trailer with Lou's weird-ass lackey Robin, whom I'd grown to despise, while he boasted to anybody who would listen about what a terrific father he was. But was I still his adored baby girl when I refused to do the new Vegas residency and refused to undertake tours?

Evidently not.

"Your dad would have completely stopped all of that," a lawyer would later remark. He could have told the physicians, "No, this is too much for my daughter, let her go home." He, however, did not.

I called my mother to ask why everyone was treating me so dangerously.

"Well, I'm not sure, I'm not sure, I'm not sure..." she'd say.

When I was in that location, I also texted my sister and requested her to get me out.

"Stop fighting it," she said via text. "There's nothing you can do about it, so stop fighting it."

She, like the rest of them, kept acting as if I was a threat in some way. This is going to sound weird, but it's the truth: I felt they were going to try to kill me. I couldn't understand how Jamie Lynn and our father had such a close relationship. She was aware that I was seeking assistance from her and that he was following me. I believed she should have sided with me.

"Britney, I had three or four nightmares when you were at that centre," one of my companions who helped me change clothes every night in the underground changing room during my Vegas run later recounted. "I'd awaken in the middle of the night. I had dreams that you committed suicide in that location. And I imagined that Robin, your so-called good assistant, called me and triumphantly declared, 'Yeah, she died in the location.'" My friend stated she was concerned about me the entire time. I was battling to stay hopeful several weeks into my stay when one of the nurses, the only one who was genuine as hell, summoned me to her computer.

"Look at this," she pointed out.

I studied her computer, trying to make sense of what I was seeing. It was a group of women on a chat show discussing me and the conservatorship. One of them was dressed in a #FreeBritney T-shirt. The nurse also showed me footage of people asking whether I was being detained somewhere against my will, talking about how much my music meant to them and how they hated to think I was suffering now. They wished to assist. And merely by doing so, they were able to assist. Everyone in the hospital was seeing everything the nurse was seeing. The doctor ultimately realised that people all around the world were wondering why I was still imprisoned. The story was all over the news. In the same way that I believe I can sense how people are feeling in Nebraska, I believe my connection to my followers helped them instinctively recognize that I was in danger. No matter where we are in space, we are connected. Even if you're on the other side of the country or the planet, we're all connected on some level. Fans of mine seemed to know despite the fact that I had stated nothing about being confined online or in the press. Seeing them marching through the streets, yelling "Free Britney!" was the most incredible sight I'd ever seen. I'm sure some folks laughed. "What kind of cause is this?" they asked, seeing the pink T-shirts with my name on them. But I don't think people would have laughed if they truly realised what I was going through and the bond I have with my followers. The truth is that I was detained without my will. And I wished to believe that people cared whether I lived or died. What do we have besides our bonds with one another? And what better way to connect than through music? Everyone who stood up for me helped me get through that difficult year, and the work they did helped me win my freedom. I don't think people realised how much the #The FreeBritney movement meant something to me at first. It meant a lot to see individuals advocating for me during the court sessions near the end. But the first time it happened, it broke my heart because I was not okay at all. And the fact that my friends and fans realised what was going on and went out of their way to help me is a debt I'll never be able to repay. Thank you from the bottom of my heart if you stood up for me when I couldn't stand up for myself. The first step toward regaining my freedom was for people to realise that I was still a real person, which I knew I could do by sharing more of my life on social media. I began trying on new clothing and posting photos of myself wearing them on Instagram. It was a lot of fun for me. Even though some people felt it was strange, I didn't mind. It feels amazing to be in complete control of the clothes and the camera after being sexualized your entire life.

I tried to reconnect with my creativity by following visual and musical artists on Instagram. I stumbled upon a guy who was making strange videos, one of which was simply a baby-pink screen with a white tiger with pink stripes roaming over it. Seeing that, I felt compelled to make something of my own, so I began experimenting with a tune. I started it out with the sound of a baby laughing. It struck me as unusual.

"Don't put a baby laughing in it!" Hesam advised.

I heeded his advice and removed it, but then another account I follow posted a video of a baby giggling, and I was jealous. That is something I should have done! I pondered. That scary laughing infant should have been my speciality!

Artists are strange, you know?

There were many people in the industry who thought I was insane at the time. At some point, I'd rather be "crazy" and be allowed to make whatever I want than "a good sport" and do what everyone tells me to do without being able to express myself. And I wanted to demonstrate my existence on Instagram. I also found myself laughing more, thanks to Amy Schumer, Kevin Hart, Sebastian Maniscalco, and Jo Koy. I admired their humour and brilliance, and how they utilise language to get under people's skin and make them laugh. That's a wonderful present. Hearing people use their voices and being themselves encouraged me that I could do the same when I uploaded videos for social media or even just in a description. Humour allowed me to avoid becoming overtaken by bitterness. I've always appreciated those with sharp wits in the entertainment sector. Laughter is the best medicine. Those may laugh because the things I share are innocent or strange, or because I can be harsh when discussing those who have wounded me. Perhaps there has been a feminist awakening. I guess what I'm saying is that the mystery of who the actual me is works in my favour—no one knows!

My children occasionally make fun of me, which I don't mind. They've always helped me shift my outlook on life. They've always seen things differently since they were children, and they're both quite creative. Sean Preston is an academic genius—he is extremely intelligent. Jayden has such a natural talent for the piano that it gives me chills. They used to join me for excellent dinners two or three nights a week before the pandemic. They were continuously showing me their great creations and telling me what they were enthused about.

"Mom, check out this painting I made!" one of them would exclaim. When I told them what I observed, they'd remark, "Yeah, but now, Mom, look at it like this." And I'd notice even more in what they'd created. I admire them for their depth and character, as much as their talent and goodness. Everything was just starting to make sense again as we entered a new decade. Then COVID struck. During the first few months of lockdown, I became even more of a homebody than I was before. I sat in my room for days, weeks, listening to self-help CDs, staring at the wall, or crafting jewellery, bored out of my mind. After I'd exhausted my supply of self-help audiobooks, I went on to storytelling audiobooks, anything labelled "Imagination"—especially anything with a British narrator.

However, out in the world, my father's security crew continued to enforce the regulations. I was on the beach one day when I removed my mask. Security came over to chastise me. I was chastised and grounded for several weeks. I didn't have Hesam with me because of the quarantines and his job schedule. I was so lonely that I started missing my family.

I called my mother and said, "I want to see you guys."

"We're shopping right now," she explained. I have to leave! We'll get back to you later."

They then didn't.

In Louisiana, the lockdown rules were different, and they were always out and about.

I eventually gave up on calling them and travelled to Louisiana to visit them. They appeared so liberated there. Why was I still talking to them? I'm not certain. Why do we continue to be in dysfunctional relationships? For one thing, I was still afraid of them, and I wanted to be friendly to them. My father was still legally my father, as he was quick to emphasise out—though I hoped not for long.

During this time with my family, I discovered that while I was in the mental health facility, they'd thrown away a lot of what I'd kept at my mother's house. My Madame Alexander dolls from childhood were all gone. My writing from the previous three years was also destroyed. I had a binder full with poems that meant a lot to me. Everything is gone.

I was overcome with melancholy when I saw the empty shelves. I remembered the pages I'd written through tears. I never intended to publish them or do anything with them, but they were significant to me. And my family had thrown them away, just like they had thrown me away.

Then I gathered my courage and reasoned, "I can get a new notebook and start over." I've been through a lot in my life. I am living today because I have experienced joy.

It was time to look for God once more.

At that moment, I made peace with my family—that is, I recognized I would never see them again, and I was okay with it.

CHAPTER 14

PURSUIT OF FREEDOM

The court-appointed lawyer who had been with me for thirteen years had never been of much assistance, but during the epidemic, I began to wonder whether I could perhaps utilise him to my advantage. I started talking to him twice a week, like a prayer, simply to think about my possibilities. Was he working for me, my father, or Lou?

I'd say to myself as he talked around the subject, "You don't seem to believe in what I know: I know where I'm going with this." I'll go all the way to the end. I can tell you're not going to finish this. Finally, I reached a tipping point. There was nothing else he could do for me. I had to take charge. I had kept quiet about the whole thing in public, but I was praying in my brain for it to end. I'm talking about genuine prayer...

So, on the evening of June 22, 2021, I dialled 911 from my residence in California to report my father for conservatorship abuse. The period in limbo between when I began pushing aggressively to stop the conservatorship and when it finally ended was difficult. I had no idea how things would turn out. Meanwhile, I couldn't say no to my father or make my own way, and it seemed like there was another documentary on me on yet another streaming service every day. This is what I was thinking when I found out my sister was writing a book. My father still had influence over me. I was powerless to defend myself. I wanted to blow up. It was difficult to see the documentaries about me. I appreciate that everyone's intentions were good, but I was offended when some old acquaintances spoke to filmmakers without first contacting me. I was astounded that someone I trusted had gone on camera. I couldn't comprehend how people could gossip about me behind my back. If that had been me, I would have called my friend to verify if it was okay to mention her. There was a lot of speculation about what I could have thought or felt.

For the previous thirteen years, I had been duped. The entire world knew I needed a new lawyer, and I eventually acknowledged it as well. It was time for me to reclaim control of my own life.

I asked my social media team and my friend Cade for assistance in locating one. This is when I brought in Mathew Rosengart, who was fantastic. He had a number of renowned clients, including Steven Spielberg and Keanu Reeves, and a lot of expertise with high-profile, tough cases as a notable former federal prosecutor now with a large legal firm. We spoke on the phone numerous times before meeting in my pool home in early July. I felt like I was getting closer to the end once Mathew was in my corner. Something had to give. It couldn't remain stationary. But, because we were dealing with the legal system, we had to do a lot of waiting and thinking.

He was shocked that I'd been refused access to a lawyer for so long. He claimed that even the most heinous criminals get to choose their own lawyers, and he detested bullying. I was relieved because I saw my father, Lou, and Robin as bullies who needed to be removed from my life.

Mathew stated that he would first go to court and file a motion to remove my father as conservator, and then it would be easier to try to cancel the entire conservatorship. Just a few weeks later, on July 26, he filed paperwork to remove my father from that position. My father was removed as my conservator after a lengthy court hearing on September 29. Before Mathew could even phone me after court, it was all over the press.

I felt a wave of relief go over me. The man who had terrified me as a child and ruled over me as an adult, who had done more than anybody else to erode my self-esteem, was no longer in charge of my life.

With my father gone, Mathew told me we had momentum, and he petitioned for the conservatorship to be lifted entirely.

In November, I was at a Tahiti resort when Mathew called to tell me that I was no longer in conservatorship. He'd promised me before I left for the vacation that one day soon I'd be able to wake up as a free woman for the first time in thirteen years. Still, I couldn't believe it when he contacted me as soon as he got out of court and told me everything was done. I was liberated.

Despite the fact that his approach had led to our win, he insisted that I take credit for what had occurred. He claimed that by testifying, I had emancipated myself and most likely benefited other persons in unfair conservatorships. After having my father take credit for everything I accomplished for so long, hearing this man say that I'd made a difference in my own life meant everything.

And now, finally, it was my turn.

Being controlled enraged me on behalf of everybody who does not have the right to choose their own fate.

"Honestly, I'm just grateful for each day... "I'm not here to be a victim," I remarked when the conservatorship ended on Instagram. "I spent my entire childhood surrounded by victims." That's why I left my residence. And laboured for twenty years, sweating profusely... "I hope my story has an impact and causes some changes in the corrupt system."

I've been attempting to reconstruct my life day by day in the months after that phone call. I'm trying to learn how to take care of myself while also having fun.

I got to do something I'd wanted to do for years while on vacation in Cancun: jet skiing. The last time I'd gone Jet Skiing was in Miami with the boys, when I went too fast attempting to keep up with them. On a Jet Ski, the kids are borderline deadly! They go at high speeds and perform jumps. Riding over the waves behind them, I crashed hard—boom, boom, boom—and fell down, tumbling out and injuring my arm.

Not wishing to go through that again, I had my assistant drive me instead in May 2022. I've discovered that having someone drive you is far superior. This time, I could feel the force of the engine, enjoy being out on the clear blue lake, and go as fast as I wanted.

That's what I'm doing now: trying to have fun but still being kind to myself and taking things at my own pace. And, for the first time in a long time, I'm giving myself permission to trust again.

I listen to music every day. I feel entirely free, completely at ease and completely pleased when I stroll about my house singing. I don't care whether I sound perfect or not. Singing, like exercise or prayer, makes me feel confident and strong. (Keep in mind that your tongue is your sword.) Anything that raises your heart rate is beneficial. Music is that, plus a link to God. That is the location of my heart.

I used to adore going to a Malibu studio when I had full-time access to one. I wrote six songs in one day. When I'm doing music for me, it's at its purest. I thought about getting a studio again and simply messing around, but I hadn't thought about recording in a long time.

I changed my mind when I was offered to record a song with Sir Elton John, a musician I've respected my entire life. He's one of my favourite artists of all time. I met him at an Oscars party about a decade ago and we hit it off right away. And now he's reached out with the sweetest video message, asking if I'd like to collaborate on one of his most renowned songs. "Hold Me Closer" would be a modernised duet version of his smash "Tiny Dancer," with elements from a couple of his other songs thrown in for good measure.

I felt very honoured. Elton John, like me, has been through a lot in public. It has given him tremendous sympathy. What a stunning man on every level.

To make the cooperation even more significant, as a child, I used to listen to "Tiny Dancer" in the vehicle on my way to and from dance and gymnastics classes in Louisiana.

Sir Elton was gracious and made me feel at ease. I went to the producer's home studio in Beverly Hills after we agreed on a recording date.

The studio was located in the house's basement. I'd never seen anything like it: a completely open studio with guitars, pianos soundboards, and music equipment. I was scared since it would be

116

the first time in six years that the world would hear my singing voice on anything fresh, but I believed in the song and in myself, so I went for it.

I took a step forward in front of the microphone, increased the tempo, and began to sing. We were finished after a few hours. On one of my favourite tracks, I recorded a duet with one of my favourite artists. In the weeks preceding up to the release, I was excited, apprehensive, and emotional.

Before the conservatory, when I went onstage, everyone looked to me for the signal that it was time to begin the performance. I'd raise my pointer finger and say, "Let's go." I was always forced to wait for everyone else during the conservatorship. I was told, "We'll let you know when we're ready." They didn't seem to regard me as having any worth. I despised it. The conservatorship had taught me to be nearly too vulnerable, too afraid. That was the cost of the conservatorship. They took a lot of my femininity, my sword, my core, my voice, and my capacity to say "Fuck you." And I realise that sounds horrible, but there is something important here. Don't underestimate your strength.

"Hold Me Closer" will be released on August 26, 2022. We were number one in forty nations by August 27. My first number one and longest-charting single in nearly a decade. And only on my terms. Complete command. Fans stated I sounded wonderful on the music. It's daunting to share your work with the rest of the world. In my experience, however, it is always worthwhile. It was an incredible pleasure to record "Hold Me Closer" and release it into the world. It didn't feel good; it felt fantastic. Moving further in my music career is not my priority right now. Now is the moment for me to strive to organise my spiritual life, to pay attention to the details, and to slow down. It's time for me to stop being someone that other people want and start being myself.I've grown to appreciate my alone time as I've become older. Being an entertainer was amazing, but my desire to amuse in front of a live audience has waned over the previous five years. I now do it for myself. When I'm alone, I feel closer to God. I'm no saint, but I know who God is. I need to do some soul-searching. It will be a long process. I'm already having fun with it.

Change is beneficial. We always pray together, Hesam and I. I look up to him because of his consistency in working out, being a decent man, being healthy, taking care of me, and teaching me how we can take care of each other. I'm grateful to him for being such an influence. The conclusion of the conservatorship was ideal for our relationship; we were allowed to start a new life together, free of restrictions, and marry. Our wedding was a lovely celebration of how far we'd come together and how much we desired for each other's happiness.

I was overcome with emotions the day the conservatorship ended: astonishment, relief, elation, sadness, and joy. I felt deceived by my father and, unfortunately, by the rest of my family as well. My sister and I should have found solace in one other, but that hasn't happened. She was writing a book about the conservatorship while I was fighting it and getting a lot of press attention. She hurriedly told me lurid things, many of which were unpleasant and ridiculous. I was quite disappointed. Shouldn't sisters be free to express their fear or vulnerability to one another without it being used as evidence of instability later on?

I couldn't get the feeling that she had no idea what I'd been through. She seemed to think it was easy for me because I had achieved so much renown so young, and she blamed me for my success and everything that came with it. Jamie Lynn was plainly suffering in our family home as well. She grew up as a divorced child, whereas I did not. She didn't appear to get a lot of parenting, and I know it was difficult for her to try to sing and act and find her own way in the world in the shadow of a sibling who received not only the majority of the family's attention, but also a lot of the world's. For all of these reasons, my heart goes out to her. But I don't think she realises how painfully poor we were before she was born. She wasn't helpless in the face of our father because of the money I brought to the family, as my mother and I were in the 1980s. When you have nothing, the pain is heightened by your inability to flee. My mother and I were forced to see the depravity and brutality without believing there was anywhere else to go. She'll always be my sister, and I adore her and her lovely family. I wish them nothing but the best. She's gone through a lot, including a teen pregnancy, divorce, and a near-fatal accident with her daughter. She's mentioned the agony of growing up in my shadow. I'm trying to be more compassionate than angry toward her and everyone else who has hurt me. It is not simple. June has told me in dreams that he knows he wounded my father, who then hurt me. I could feel his affection and see how he'd changed on the other side. I hope to be able to feel better about the rest of my family one day.

My rage has manifested physically, particularly in the form of migraine migraines. When I get them, I don't want to go to the doctor since being sent from one doctor to the next for so long has given me a phobia of them. As a result, I handle things myself. When it comes to migraines, I don't like to talk about them because I'm afraid it will make them worse.

I can't go into the light and I can't move when I have one. In the dark, I maintain complete stillness. Any light causes my head to throb and makes me feel dizzy—it's that awful. I'll be sleeping for a day and a half. I'd never had a headache in my life until recently. When my brother complained about his headaches, I assumed he was exaggerating how awful they were. I'm sorry I ever said anything to cast doubt on him.

A migraine is worse than stomach sickness in my opinion. With a bug, you can still think clearly. Your mind can assist you decide what you want to do and what movies to watch. When you get a migraine, however, you are unable to function since your brain is absent. Migraines are only one aspect of the physical and mental trauma I've suffered since being released from conservatorship. I don't believe my family realises the extent of their actions.

For thirteen years, I couldn't eat what I wanted, drive, spend my money as I wanted, or even drink coffee. The freedom to do anything I want has restored my femininity. In my forties, I'm experiencing things for the first time. I feel like the lady in me has been suppressed for far too long. I'm finally roaring back to life. I might be able to sin in Sin City as well.

For the first time in many years, I've begun to appreciate the benefits of being an adult woman. I feel like I've been underwater for a long time, only sometimes swimming to the surface to gulp for oxygen and a bite to eat. When I regained my freedom, it was my cue to go onto dry land—and to take vacations, sip a cocktail, drive my car, visit a resort, or gaze out at the ocean whenever I wanted. I've been taking things day by day and trying to be grateful for the little things. I'm grateful that my father is no longer in my life. I no longer have to be afraid of him. If I gain weight, it'll be a relief to know that no one will be screaming at me, "You need to pick it up!" I got to eat chocolate once more. My body got strong and my fire returned as soon as my father was no longer present to force me to consume what he wanted me to eat. I felt more confident, and I began to like how I looked again. On Instagram, I enjoy dressing up.

Many people don't understand why I enjoy photographing myself naked or in new clothes. But I think if they'd been shot hundreds of times by other people, prodded and positioned for other people's approval, they'd realise that I get a lot of delight from posing the way I feel sexy and taking my own picture, doing anything I want with it. I was born nude into this world, and I truly believe the weight of the world has been placed on my shoulders. I wanted to see myself as lighter and more liberated. I had my entire life in front of me as a baby, and that's how I feel now, like a blank slate.

I truly believe I have been reincarnated. I adore the sense of the voice leaving my body and bouncing back at me when I sing while I move around at home, exactly like I did when I was a little kid. I'm finding the joy again of why I wanted to sing to begin with. That sensation is sacred to me. I do it for me and no one else.

I'm constantly asked when I'm going to put on another concert. I'll admit that I'm stumped by that question. I'm dancing and singing like I used to when I was younger, not for the benefit of my family or to get something, but for myself and my real enjoyment of it.

Only now do I feel like I'm regaining my confidence in other people and in God. I know what makes me happy and joyful. I attempt to dwell on the places and concepts that allow me to have that experience. Beautiful places, my sons, my husband, my friends, and my pets are all things I enjoy. I adore my followers.

When it comes to admirers, they occasionally inquire about my special bond with the gay community.

It's all about love—unconditional love—for me. My gay buddies were constantly protective of me, perhaps because they understood I was somewhat naïve. Not stupid, but far too nice. And I believe many of the gay men around me were supportive. I could even feel it onstage while they were standing next to me. If I didn't think I gave my greatest performance, I could count on my friends to notice and yet exclaim, "You did so good!" That type of affection means the world to me.

My favourite nights were when I went out with my dancers. We went to a homosexual bar in Europe once, and I felt like everyone on the dance floor was so tall. I enjoyed the club's excellent electro dance music. I danced until six o'clock in the morning and it felt like two seconds. My heart was racing. It was a spiritual experience to be with individuals who I could feel loved me unreservedly, similar to the mystical time in Arizona. It doesn't matter what you do, say, or who you know when you have pals like that. That is genuine love.

I recall going to a showcase in Italy when several drag artists sang my tunes. It was incredible. The painters were stunning. They were completely immersed in the moment, and I could tell they enjoyed performing. They had a lot of passion and determination, which I admire.

When I was released from the conservatorship, I was able to visit the two holiday spots that I had missed, Maui and Cancun. I swam in the ocean, sat in the sun, played with Sawyer, my new puppy, and went on boat excursions with Hesam. I read extensively before writing this book. I discovered I was pregnant while on the road. I'd desired another child for a long time. Hesam and I had wanted to create our own family for a long time. I admire him for his stability. I adore the fact that he does not even drink. He is a divine gift. And learning that Chris and I were expecting our first child together made me ecstatic.

I, too, was terrified. I was depressed during my pregnancy with Sean Preston and Jayden. This pregnancy was similar in many ways—I was a little unwell and liked food and sex—and I worried if the sadness would return as well. I did notice that I was moving a little slower. I prefer to be up and about. But because my life was so much better and I had so much support, I was convinced I could get through it.

I miscarried before the end of my first trimester. I'd been so excited to be pregnant that I'd informed everyone, which meant I had to un-tell everyone. "It is with great sadness that we must inform you that we have lost our miracle baby early in the pregnancy," we wrote on Instagram. This is a difficult time for any parent. Perhaps we should have waited until we were farther along before announcing. We were, nonetheless, overjoyed to convey the good news. Our strength comes from our affection for one another. We will continue to try to grow our wonderful family. We appreciate all of your assistance. We respectfully request privacy during this difficult time."

I was saddened by the loss of the baby. But, once again, music assisted me in gaining understanding and perspective. Every song I sing or dance to allows me to convey a different story and provides a fresh avenue for me to escape. Listening to music on my phone helps me deal with the anger and despair that come with being an adult. I try not to worry about my family too much these days, but I'm curious what they'll think of this book. Because I was suppressed for thirteen years, I wonder if they've ever thought, Maybe she's right, when they see me speaking out. I believe they have a guilty conscience, that they realise deep down that what they did to me was wrong. All those years of doing what I was told and being treated in a specific way have taught me what kinds of people I want to be around and who I don't. Much of the media has been unkind to me, and this hasn't changed just because I'm no longer in conservatorship. There has been much conjecture regarding how I am doing. I know my fans are concerned. I am now free. I'm simply being myself and attempting to mend. I can finally do what I want, when I want. And I don't take anything for granted.

On social media, freedom means being foolish and ridiculous. Freedom means being able to take a break from Instagram without having to contact 911. Freedom entails the ability to make mistakes and learn from them. I'm free because I don't have to perform for anyone, on or offstage. Freedom allows me to be as delightfully flawed as everyone else. And freedom entails the opportunity and right to seek joy in my own way, on my own terms. It took a long time and a great deal of effort for me to feel ready to relate my tale. I hope it inspires people and touches their hearts in some way. Since I've been free, I've had to create an entirely new identity. I've had to remind myself, "Wait a minute, this is who I was—someone passive and pleasing." A girl. And this is who I am now: someone strong and self-assured. A lady. I had grandiose fantasies when I was a little child, laying on the warm rocks in my neighbour's garden. I felt composed and in command. I was confident that I could make my aspirations come true. I didn't always have the power to make the world seem the way I wanted it to for a long time, but I do now in many ways. I can't alter the past, but I no longer have to feel lonely or afraid. I've gone through a lot since I was a kid wandering the Louisiana woods. I've written music, toured the world, become a mother, found and lost love, and found it again. I hadn't been genuinely present in my own life, in my own strength, in my womanhood in a long time. But now I'm here.

Printed in Great Britain
by Amazon

33517618R10069